Praise for *Mastering Interest Rate Risk Strategy*

'*Mastering Interest Rate Risk Strategy* is a wonderful and easy to read tour of interest rate risk and its management, and mismanagement, by non-financial firms. Starting with some of the recent large derivative blunders, the book then deftly walks the reader through the basic theory on how to best understand, measure and manage interest rate risk in a very user friendly way. Anyone who wants to better understand why and how non-financial firms should be dealing with interest rate risk should read this book.'

Gordon M. Bodnar, Morris W. Offit Professor on International Finance, Johns Hopkins University, USA

'Macrae's guide is an excellent cookbook for financial managers that want to manage interest rate risks.The hands-on RISK method by Macrae is an academically sound and practically useful approach to manage the interest rate risks in your company. With the blunders we have witnessed in the use of derivatives in the past decades, now it's time that financial managers study Macrae's new book in interest rate risk management. With many cases and examples, this book offers guidance in robust risk management techniques.'

Abe de Jong, Professor of Corporate Finance and Corporate Governance, Rotterdam School of Management, Erasmus University

'The section on MiFID I and MiFID II, which covers the core legal aspects of customer protection with respect to derivatives advisory and sales, is a clear and easily readable piece that financial professionals dealing with interest rate risk derivatives should be aware of.'

Harman Korte, board member of The Netherlands Authority for the Financial Markets

'Mastering interest rate risk management is a core capability of treasury. This comprehensive book brings together both knowledge and best practices in this area. A must-read for financial professionals.'

Klaas A. Springer, Corporate Treasurer of FrieslandCampina

Mastering Interest Rate Risk Strategy

Mastering Interest Rate Risk Strategy

A practical guide to managing corporate financial risk

VICTOR MACRAE

PEARSON

Harlow, England • London • New York • Boston • San Francisco • Toronto • Sydney
Auckland • Singapore • Hong Kong • Tokyo • Seoul • Taipei • New Delhi
Cape Town • São Paulo • Mexico City • Madrid • Amsterdam • Munich • Paris • Milan

PEARSON EDUCATION LIMITED

Edinburgh Gate
Harlow CM20 2JE
United Kingdom
Tel: +44 (0)1279 623623
Web: www.pearson.com/uk

First edition published 2015 (print and electronic)

ISBN: 978-1-292-01756-3 (print)
978-1-292-01758-7 (PDF)
978-1-292-01759-4 (ePub)
978-1-292-01757-0 (eText)

British Library Cataloguing-in-Publication Data
A catalogue record for the print edition is available from the British Library

Library of Congress Cataloging-in-Publication Data
Macrae, Victor.
Mastering interest rate risk strategy : a practical guide to managing corporate financial risk / Victor Macrae. -- 1st Edition.
pages cm
Includes bibliographical references and index.
ISBN 978-1-292-01756-3
1. Interest rate risk. 2. Corporations--Finance--Management. 3. Derivative securities. I. Title.
HG6024.5.M33 2015
658.15'5--dc23

2015008175

10 9 8 7 6 5 4 3 2 1
19 18 17 16 15

Print edition typeset in 11.5pt Garamond by 3

NOTE THAT ANY PAGE CROSS REFERENCES REFER TO THE PRINT EDITION

Contents

Acknowledgements

The conception of a book is largely a question of the inspiration of the writer. That having been said, receiving support is essential for various reasons. If you are totally immersed in the subject, it is necessary once in a while to be confronted by outsiders. Working together with others also strongly motivated me as I could set deadlines for myself, accelerating the writing process, and needless to say a fresh pair of eyes reviewing my book was a tremendous impetus.

I want to thank all the people who have shown their interest during the writing process, and the following in particular. My wife Marianne was very supportive in helping me choose the right path when a choice had to be made. I asked her 'I have some alternatives, which one do you think is best?' The issue was instantly solved. My father Sandy, a native English speaker, has done a great job in improving the English. I'm Scottish but was raised as a Dutch speaker. Unfortunately, English has therefore remained a second language. Even the sometimes minor changes that he suggested had a great impact.

I'm very grateful to Louise Cornelis and Bianca Minkman for their invaluable contributions. Louise has been a great help in structuring the book so that the reader can more readily follow my train of thought. Bianca has made the book more readable by her suggestions that bring more life to the sometimes dry theory.

Many thanks to two professionals who have dedicated some of their time to proofread the book. As an academic, Robin Litjens has attentively pointed out issues needing further clarification. Lex van der Wielen, a financial markets professional, suggested improvements to the section on derivatives. I take full responsibility for any remaining errors.

Last but not least I would like to express my gratitude to my editor Christopher Cudmore. We were discussing the contents of this book long before the first word was written. He helped me sharpen my thoughts and improve my writing style. Finally, he had faith in the realisation of this book from the outset. Thanks Chris!

About the author

Victor Macrae (www.victormacrae.com) has a Ph.D. in corporate financial risk management. He has worked in the financial world for more than twenty years and has encountered interest rate risk from different perspectives: as a treasurer at listed publishing company Wolters Kluwer, as a project financier at ING (Barings) and as a consultant at his own company Macrae Finance, which he founded in 2006.

At Wolters Kluwer Victor was responsible for managing interest rate risk and overseeing the inception of IFRS. As a consultant Victor executed various projects for firms to establish an optimal strategy for financial risk management. He also screened treasury sales departments of banks and ran consulting projects to optimise derivatives sales practices.

Based on his Ph.D. research and on his vast practical experience, Victor developed an analytical method for establishing an optimal interest rate risk strategy. He used it for consulting and training purposes and has licensed it to third parties. Victor has trained several treasury sales departments of (international) banks on the basis of this analytical method. He has also performed numerous assessments of the knowledge and correct use of the method by derivatives sales advisors. In this book Victor shares his knowledge on interest rate risk management and the analytical method with you.

Building on his infrastructure project finance experience at ING, Victor also focuses on investment projects. For instance, for energy company Alliander he set up an investment fund for investing in sustainable energy projects.

Victor pursued business studies at BBA, MSc and MBA level (Nyenrode University) and delved into strategy consulting (Rotterdam School of Management). He acts as speaker (Dutch Association of Corporate Treasurers) and gives presentations (BDO). He publishes in financial newspapers and journals and is a columnist on treasury issues for the Dutch financial magazine *Controllers Magazine*.

Preface

In recent years we've seen many newspaper headlines reporting the mis-selling of interest rate derivatives and costly derivatives blunders. A key reason for these is that people don't have a complete understanding of a firm's interest rate risk and of the risks arising from the use of derivatives. The aim of this book is to solve that problem.

When encountering interest rate risk at the corporate treasury of firms, at banks, in consulting and in the academic world, I didn't have a comprehensive analytical method that would support the establishment of a sound interest rate risk strategy. On the basis of my Ph.D. research on corporate financial risk management I decided to construct one. My goal was to establish a method that was academically sound but also practical.

I first tested the analytical method when advising firms on their interest rate risk management strategy. I reasoned that if I could use it for my own analysis and at the same time use it to explain interest rate risk strategy to non-experts such as controllers and heads of administration, it would be practical enough. Secondly I trained treasury sales advisors of banks to use the analytical method. These derivatives sales persons already have a lot of experience in this discipline. Nevertheless, they were very positive about the analytical method, commenting that it enhanced their understanding of managing interest rate risk from the perspective of the firm and gave them a good structure for analysis. Thirdly I formalised the analytical method. It was licensed to a bank and incorporated in a worldwide training manual.

In the meantime I have upgraded the graphics and added strategy consulting techniques to enhance the method and to make it more easily transferable. I also registered it as a trademark under the name: The Macrae RISK Reduction Rules®. RISK is an acronym that stands for:

- Risk formulation: The main goal of step 1 is to formulate the risk issue of the firm. The further steps of the analytical method are designed to provide an optimal answer to this risk issue.

- Impact analysis: The main goal of step 2 is to determine the value of risk management.
- Scenario analysis: The main goal of step 3 is to determine in what ways the firm's risk can be managed, with or without derivatives.
- Knowledge application: The best strategy for risk management is determined from the alternatives provided in step 3. The main goal of step 4 is to formulate an answer to the risk issue defined in step 1.

Mastering Interest Rate Risk Strategy is to my knowledge the first comprehensive guide that will provide insight into how to establish an interest rate risk strategy for non-financial firms. I hope it will contribute to more profitable business, fewer derivatives blunders and less mis-selling of derivatives.

Victor Macrae

Introduction

If this were a textbook I would have started by explaining the techniques used for managing interest rate risk, followed by an analysis of past derivatives blunders and concluding with the analytical method for establishing an optimal interest rate risk strategy. However, as this is a practical guide for financial professionals, I assume that you have at the very least a basic knowledge of the subject. I wanted to make the book more interesting and valuable for you by starting with how not to do it! It therefore begins with past derivatives disasters. A great advantage of this approach is that rather than treating these disasters in isolation we can use these past errors as learning points throughout the whole book.

Mastering Interest Rate Risk Strategy is about formulating an optimal interest rate risk management strategy from a firm's perspective. It consists of six parts. Part 1 is a prelude to the rest of the book in order to understand what can go wrong if you don't formulate an optimal interest rate risk strategy. It sets the scene and provides insight into the origins of derivatives blunders. The learning points from Part 1 are intertwined with the other five parts of the book. Parts 2 to 5 provide you with detailed background information on a firm's interest rate risk management process and form the building blocks for Part 6. In Part 6 I show you the analytical method for formulating an optimal firm-specific strategy for managing interest rate risk and assume that you have grasped the underlying concepts in Parts 2 to 5.

The structure of the book is as follows:

- Part 1 shows you the many pitfalls of managing interest rate risk with derivatives.
- Parts 2, 3, 4 and 5 give you the background theory you need to thoroughly understand the topic.
- Part 6 puts it all together and enables you to formulate an optimal interest rate risk strategy.

Parts 2, 3, 4 and 5 follow the natural sequence of a firm's interest rate risk management process:

1. The firm's exposure to interest rate risk (discussed in Part 2).
2. The influence of the variable interest rate on the firm's financial statements (Part 3).
3. The creation of the firm's value by hedging (Part 4).
4. The use of derivatives to hedge interest rate risk (Part 5).

This book focuses on understanding the interest rate risk of a non-financial firm, which is different from that of a financial firm. Whereas a corporate can benefit from mitigating interest rate risk, a financial firm may actively seek interest rate risk in order to make a profit.

The premise of the analytical method is that hedging interest rate risk creates value for the firm. This is the reason that we explore into hedging theory in Part 4. This theory is sometimes dry but it's necessary to understand the reasons why a firm can benefit from hedging.

This book is not about hedge accounting (IFRS). However, if you follow the steps of the analytical method in Part 6, the likelihood of qualifying for hedge accounting strongly increases because in line with IFRS the method is set up to mitigate risk.

Last but not least, the catch-22 situation is that the use of a derivative, which is basically an instrument to mitigate risk, at the same time increases risk. The biggest problem seems to be that many people are either not aware of (all) the risks or that they are underestimated. The European Union has issued 'The Directive on Markets in Financial Instruments' (MiFID I & II) which includes regulations on customer protection regarding derivatives advice and sales by banks and investment firms. In Appendix III MiFID is investigated. Irrespective of regulations, I hope that this book enhances the knowledge and skills of all financial professionals who encounter interest rate risk in their work.

Part 1

KEY LEARNING POINTS FROM PAST DERIVATIVES BLUNDERS

INTRODUCTION TO PART 1

In corporate interest rate risk management there are few natural ways to mitigate risk in comparison to foreign exchange risk management. In other words, in establishing an optimal strategy to manage interest rate risk the use of derivatives is quite common. With derivatives interest rate risk can be decreased, but also (unintentionally) increased.

In this section we're going to look at derivatives blunders made by firms when they manage interest rate risk. The aim is to show you what can go wrong with derivatives so that you won't make the same mistakes. I have analysed past derivatives blunders and have looked for the common features that have caused them. I'll link the derivatives blunders discussed here to the interest rate derivatives that are discussed in Part 5 so that you are aware of the specific dangers of using certain derivatives. Furthermore, if you follow the steps of the analytical method in Part 6 on formulating an optimal interest rate risk strategy, you will avoid making derivatives blunders.

It's important to bear in mind that the focus is on derivatives blunders made by firms that use interest rate derivatives. Derivatives blunders made by financial institutions are not taken into account. Derivatives blunders other than regarding interest rate risk, such as with respect to foreign exchange rate risk or commodity risk, are also disregarded.

As many derivatives blunders and accusations of mis-selling of derivatives are based on interest rate swaps, most examples used in this part are based on the situation where a firm has a variable rate loan in combination with an interest rate swap.

1

Corporate derivatives blunders

Newspaper headlines

Five main categories of derivatives blunders

NEWSPAPER HEADLINES

These derivatives blunders have caused a lot of commotion. I'll share some newspaper headlines with you.

Newspaper headlines

'Former Porsche executives to stand trial', *Financial Times*, 26 August 2014

'... Two former Porsche executives must stand trial over the sports car maker's failed attempt to take over Volkswagen, a Stuttgart court has ruled, paving the way for one of the most keenly awaited cases in German corporate history. Wendelin Wiedeking and Holger Härter, respectively Porsche's former chief executive and chief financial officer, were charged in 2012 with "information-based market manipulation" in relation to Porsche's attempt to acquire VW via a complex and secretive options strategy ...'

'Dutch housing sector in crisis over Vestia's €20bn rate swap gamble', *Social Housing Magazine*, 8 March 2012

'... The Netherlands' biggest affordable housing provider is facing break-up and seeking billions of pounds in financial guarantees from the rest of the sector after losing €2.5 billion in a derivatives deal. Vestia, which owns 89,000 units and is based in Rotterdam, faces a €2.5 billion margin call on €20 billion-worth of interest rate swaps ...'

'Four vocational training colleges latest to join derivatives scandal', *DutchNews.nl*, 27 July 2012

'... Four large vocational college groups are the latest public institutions to have become embroiled in the derivatives scandal, the *Telegraaf* reports on Friday ... The Midden Nederland and West-Brabant ROC groups, the Zadkine group and the Albelda College in Rotterdam have all invested heavily in interest-rate derivatives in an effort to offset the cost of loans to build new buildings, the paper says ... The *Financieele Dagblad* reported on Monday Amsterdam's VU university and Leiden University may lose millions of euros because of their reliance on derivatives ...'

FIVE MAIN CATEGORIES OF DERIVATIVES BLUNDERS

There are a significant number of corporate interest rate derivatives blunders from which we can learn how not to do it. Based on my research for this book, I have constructed five main categories of derivatives blunders that are similar to each other. Each category includes one or more subcategories.

Table 1.1 **The five categories of derivatives blunders**

	Category of derivatives blunders	Problem	Effects
1	Deliberate speculation with derivatives	No underlying exposure	Cash necessary to pay margin calls Cash necessary to meet interest payments
2	Overhedging with derivatives	Mismatch between the principal of the derivative and the principal of the underlying exposure	Probably no qualification for hedge accounting; changes in the value of the derivative are pure profit or loss
		Mismatch between the term of the derivative and the term of the underlying exposure	Probably no qualification for hedge accounting; changes in the value of the derivative are pure profit or loss
3	Interest payable remains variable with derivatives	Interest markup can be increased	Interest payable is not fixed
4	Negative value of derivatives	The owner of the firm wants to sell the firm or discontinue its activities	Cash necessary to settle the negative value of derivatives
		The firm early (partially) repays the underlying loan	Cash necessary to settle the negative value of derivatives
		The bank runs higher risk on the firm	Liquidity squeeze
5	Link between derivative and underlying loan	Switching banks requires additional liquidity	Refinancing must be sufficient to cover the loan repayment and the negative value of the derivative

There is a difference between the first category of derivatives blunders, deliberate speculation with derivatives, and the four other categories where the intention is to mitigate risk. Nevertheless, whatever the category of derivatives blunders, the effects can be disastrous.

I've given an overview in Table 1.1 of the five categories of derivatives blunders. For each derivative blunder I have stated the core of the underlying problem and the effects on the firm.

I'm now going to discuss each category in detail. The examples that are used are mainly based on the combination of a variable rate term loan or working capital facility and an interest rate swap. The reason for doing this is that past derivatives blunders have often been caused by this specific combination because they were often sold as a substitute for a fixed rate loan.

1. Deliberate speculation with derivatives

With deliberate speculation with derivatives the intention is to take a gamble with derivatives based on a personal view of future interest rate movements. It is not the intention to hedge an exposure. Rather, risk is knowingly taken by entering into an open derivatives position without an underlying position.

Whereas deliberate risk taking with derivatives may be part of the business of a financial institution or hedge fund, corporates generally engage in derivatives with a view to mitigating risk. However, there are some exceptions: some corporates do engage in derivatives speculation. The two examples below show what can happen if it all goes wrong.

The main goal of speculation is clear: to make a profit. However, the underlying reasons may vary, as you will read in the incredible stories about two accomplished corporates that start speculating with modest amounts and end up spending unbelievable sums that by far exceed their business operations:

1. World's greatest corporate loss due to speculation: housing corporation Vestia.
2. A failed takeover of the world's second largest car manufacturer: sports car manufacturer Porsche.

Example

Deliberate speculation: housing corporation Vestia[1]

World's greatest corporate loss due to speculation

Vestia is the largest housing corporation in The Netherlands. It has only one director: Erik Staal. Its treasurer is Marcel de Vries.

Marcel de Vries has the reputation of being an expert in the area of derivatives. He lectures on derivatives and is seen as an example of how housing corporations should manage their finances. All derivative transactions are controlled by De Vries himself. Erik Staal signs the derivatives contracts. All derivatives transactions are administered by De Vries in an Excel spreadsheet! There is no risk manager nor any consultation with directors or supervisors. Only one employee forms the 'back office'.

At the end of 2010 De Vries believes that interest rates have fallen to a low and are sure to increase. Furthermore, in 2011 the financial guidelines at Vestia are changed to accommodate open derivatives positions. In order to benefit maximally from his interest rate view, De Vries enters into additional interest rate derivatives. Without the knowledge of their supervisors, De Vries and Staal speculate with swaps, caps, floors and other exotic financial products. For instance, swaptions are sold. The option premiums received are used to lower the interest payable in structured interest rate swaps. In contrast to De Vries' personal view, interest rates further decrease. In a panic, De Vries increases the stakes in order to make good the loss. By then, Vestia has more than 400 derivatives contracts with a principal value of €23 billion! Only 20% thereof have underlying loans. 80% is pure speculation!

As a result of the further drop in market interest rates, and therefore the further increase of the negative market value of the derivatives, in September 2011 Vestia has to deposit more than €1 billion in margin call. Just before Christmas a second margin call of €500 million is due. The Dutch government is informed of the precarious situation. At the end of January 2012 Vestia has to deposit another margin call of €500 million. This time Vestia has run out of cash and is unable to do so. The Dutch government intervenes and Erik Staal is dismissed. On 19 June 2012 Vestia and the banks agree to settle the entire derivatives portfolio: total settlement costs add up to €2 billion!

The loss of Vestia due to derivatives speculation is the largest worldwide corporate loss that has ever occurred!

Deliberate speculation: sports car manufacturer Porsche[2,3]

Example

A failed takeover of the world's second largest car manufacturer

Porsche is a German family-owned sports car manufacturer. In 2005 Porsche's CEO Wendelin Wiedeking and CFO Holger Härter devise a bold plan to take over Volkswagen by acquiring 75% of its listed shares. Not only is Volkswagen the world's second largest car manufacturer, it is also 14 times larger than Porsche and produces 60 times more cars!

At that point in time Porsche has €3 billion in cash and is very profitable. Business is booming. Profit is not distributed to the owners but remains within the company. As a result the cash pile increases. Porsche has no debt. However, debt is easy to obtain. The strategy for financing the takeover is to attract loans next to using the liquidity available. Nevertheless, these measures do not generate sufficient cash to acquire 75% of Volkswagen shares. Therefore, Porsche comes up with a devious plan to generate additional cash by buying call options and selling put options. The extra cash generated with the options is invested in Volkswagen shares. Porsche has an attractive perspective: when it has control over Volkswagen, it can use Volkswagen's well stocked wallet with €13 billion in cash to repay all its debt at once.

The rationale behind buying call options is to ensure that at expiration the share price is above the strike price of the option. In that case Porsche receives the difference between the share price and the strike price in cash. The idea behind selling put options is to ensure that at expiration the share price is higher than the strike price. Porsche can then use the option premium (cash) to purchase Volkswagen shares. Thus, Porsche speculates with both call and put options on the share price of Volkswagen increasing. Because Porsche continuously purchases Volkswagen shares, there is ongoing demand for the share and the price increases.

The speculation with call and put options increases spectacularly. In 2005 Porsche pays option premiums of around €510 million and receives €780 million. Thus, Porsche earns €270 million through speculation. In 2006/07 Porsche pays option premiums of €3.3 billion, six times the amount of the previous year. Profit is €3 billion. In 2008/09 Porsche pays an unbelievable sum of €56.1 billion in option premiums. This is more than Porsche has earned with the sale of sports cars in the past decennium! As a result of the option speculation, Porsche's profit in 2007/08 is higher than ▶

its turnover! Turnover is €7.46 billion and profit peaks at €8.57 billion. Profit from operational activities, the sale of sports cars, is 'merely' €1 billion. The rest is due to the option constructions. Between 2005 and 2009 Porsche has probably gained a total profit with option speculation of €8.23 billion!

In 2008 Porsche has loans totalling €3 billion. Interest on the loans is approximately 5%, as a result of which interest payments yearly are around €150 million. At this point in time interest payments can be easily generated by the operations of Porsche.

The largest financial risks are that the share price of Volkswagen strongly decreases and that the banks withdraw the credit lines. Unfortunately, in September 2008 a global financial crisis erupts. Due to the crisis it becomes increasingly difficult for Porsche to finance the acquisition and to pay the interest on its loans. At the start of 2009, in the middle of the crisis, Porsche draws an additional €6 billion under a credit line totalling €10 billion to buy more Volkswagen shares. As a result, Porsche has a 50.8% stake in Volkswagen.

Interest on the debt amounts to around €600 million. It is a serious battle for Porsche to raise the yearly interest payments. Furthermore, due to the large loan, Porsche is completely dependent on the banks. Because of the crisis, the banks are more critical about the ability of Porsche to take over Volkswagen and to acquire Volkswagen's cash in order to repay Porsche's massive debt. Porsche is in an awkward position: its chances of taking control of Volkswagen have severely weakened, it has huge debts and its car sales are under strong pressure. Porsche needs help.

The unbelievable happens and the roles reverse. The predator becomes the prey: Porsche is not able to survive without the help of Volkswagen. Finally, in July 2009, Porsche is sold to Volkswagen and loses its autonomy.

Were Vestia and Porsche victims of external circumstances only? It doesn't seem that way. Evidence shows that the personal incentives of the key players encouraged excessive risk taking.

Newspaper headlines **'Topman Vestia opgepakt', *Telegraaf*, 14 April 2012**

Translation: 'Vestia chief arrested'

'... Vestia financial chief Marcel de V. of housing corporation Vestia was arrested on suspicion of bribery and money laundering ... He is suspected of bribery through receiving 'kickback fees' from a middle man that advised Vestia in investing in financial products ...'

'Ousted Porsche chief receives €50m pay-off as families agree VW merger', *Financial Times*, 24 July 2009

'... One of the best-paid managers in the world, Mr Wiedeking was accused by one politician of "cashing in big time" ... In a move to avert a growing public outcry, Mr Wiedeking, who has earned almost €80m in the past financial year, said that he would give half the pay-off to charity and most of that amount to a newly formed charity for Porsche employees ...'

Vestia entered into derivatives contracts with banks through a small financial consultancy. The consultancy required banks to pay fees for the derivatives contracts. Treasurer De Vries 'asked' the consultancy for part of the fees, which were secretly transferred to him. One of the partners of the consultancy became anxious and talked to the police. As a result De Vries was accused of fraud and corruption. Over the years the financial consultancy is believed to have generated €20 million in fees of which allegedly half is passed to De Vries. Personal gain may therefore play an important role in the behaviour of De Vries. Staal was not part of these secret transactions and was not aware of their existence.

As CEO of Porsche Wendelin Wiedeking received a stiff bonus of 0.9% of Porsche's profits. He led Porsche over a period of 17 years. In his last years, as a result of the option speculations, he is said to have received between €50 and €80 million in remuneration. Since he speculated with the money of the owners of Porsche, financially he had a lot to gain and little to lose. This may partly explain the enormous risks he took.

Key issues of derivatives blunders

Deliberate speculation

- Both Vestia and Porsche are fascinating examples that show how pure speculation with derivatives can turn into a disaster.
- In both cases it was a lack of (access to) cash that led to failure, even though the mechanisms were slightly different. In the case of Vestia it was a lack of cash to meet the margin calls. In the case of Porsche it was lack of cash to meet the interest payments and loan repayments.

- Speculating with derivatives may be tempting sometimes. However, if you ever have such a thought, be aware and think of Vestia and Porsche!

2. Overhedging with derivatives

The second category of derivatives blunders concerns overhedging. This is a situation where the principal of the derivative is higher than the principal of the underlying exposure, such as a loan in the case of interest rate risk.

Overhedging

$$\frac{\text{Principal derivative}}{\text{Principal underlying exposure}} > 100\%$$

In the case of overhedging the same situation arises as with speculation: an open derivatives position without an underlying asset or liability. The difference is that with pure speculation the open position is actively sought whereas with overhedging the open position arises by accident.

Overhedging can occur because of two reasons:

1. Mismatch between the principal of the derivative and the principal of the underlying exposure.
2. Mismatch between the term of the derivative and the term of the underlying exposure.

1. Mismatch between the principal of the derivative and the principal of the underlying exposure

In order to constitute a hedge, the principal of the underlying loan should be at least equal to or higher than the principal of the derivative. A principal mismatch arises when the principal of the derivative is higher than the principal of the underlying loan. This mismatch can have different sources and can arise at different moments during the life of the derivative.

There are four reasons why a principal mismatch can occur:

1. There is an original match between the principal of the derivative and the principal of the underlying exposure, but the underlying exposure does not materialise as expected.

2. The principal of the derivative is not aligned with the debt redemption schedule of the underlying loan.
3. Early repayment of the underlying loan is not synchronised with the principal of the derivative.
4. The amount drawn under the underlying loan is less than expected.

Examples of principal mismatch

Example

The underlying exposure does not materialise as expected

A university wants to build a new building. For financing, it opts for a variable rate loan in combination with an interest rate swap. In order to fully hedge interest rate risk, the principal and term of the interest rate swap match that of the underlying loan. The university enters into the interest rate swap agreement and believes it has prudently hedged interest rate risk. Unfortunately, due to changing market circumstances resulting in the board of directors taking a new strategy, the new building is no longer necessary. The building contract is cancelled. As the interest rate swap agreement is already signed, an open derivative position now exists as the interest rate swap has no underlying exposure any more. The university will have to sell the interest rate swap and pay or receive its market value. Furthermore, it will have to pay transaction costs again.

Example

The principal of the derivative is not aligned with the debt redemption schedule of the underlying loan

A producer of technical machinery has a loan agreement with its bank based on a variable interest rate. The firm has benefited from low market rates, but now interest rates are rising and the firm expects further market rate increases in the future. The firm decides to hedge interest rate risk by purchasing an interest rate swap that matches the principal of the underlying loan. A year later part of the loan is repaid according to the debt redemption schedule. Unfortunately, the debt redemption schedule was not taken into account when the derivative was purchased: as a result an open derivatives position arises for the repaid part of the loan.

Example

Early repayment of the underlying loan is not synchronised with the principal of the derivative

An accounting firm has a long-term loan with a variable interest rate in combination with an interest rate swap. The parameters of the swap match the parameters of the underlying loan. Business is booming. The firm generates excess cash and wants to use the proceeds for early debt repayment. Consequently, after the early repayment the principal of the swap exceeds the principal of the loan.

Example

The amount drawn under the underlying loan is less than expected

An international trade firm has a working capital facility. In order to be certain about future interest payments, it has fixed the variable market interest rate through an interest rate swap for half the principal of the working capital facility. The firm has estimated that this is the core of the working capital facility that it will always need. However, due to unexpected fierce competition, the firm expects to sell fewer products and therefore it severely cuts its purchases. As a consequence the debt drawn is lower than the estimated core level and a partially open derivatives position arises.

2. Mismatch between the term of the derivative and the term of the underlying exposure

A derivative hedges the underlying loan if the term of the derivative is the same or shorter than the term of the loan. If the term of the derivative is longer than the term of the loan, there is no hedge but an open derivatives position.

Example

The term of the derivative is longer than the term of the underlying loan

A trade firm has a working capital facility based on a variable market interest rate. A five-year interest rate swap covers the core need of the working capital facility. Currently, the remaining term of the interest rate swap is three years. Unfortunately, the company has performed poorly due to adverse market conditions and has breached the covenants in the financing agreement. The working capital facility can be cancelled on a daily basis and the bank is not willing to prolong the facility. As a result an open derivatives position is created.

The consequence of a (partly) open derivatives position due to principal or term mismatch is threefold:

1. There is an open position with an opposite risk: in the examples above the firm intends to hedge the risk that the short-term interest rate increases. However, for the overhedged part the risk is that the long-term interest rate decreases.
2. If a derivative does not constitute a hedge, under IFRS and under national accounting regulations that have adopted (part) of IFRS, market value changes have to be accounted for in the profit and loss account.
3. If the firm wants to solve the (partly) open derivatives position, it will have to pay transaction costs again.

A third class of mismatch exists: a combination of a principal and term overhedge. I won't provide examples as they are combinations of the instances above.

Key issues of derivatives blunders

Overhedging with derivatives

All five examples are errors of judgement in varying degrees:

- In the first example using an interest rate swap probably wasn't the right choice of derivative: the university could have used swaptions, an option on an interest rate swap.
- In the second and fifth examples a technical error occurred: a debt redemption schedule should be considered to prevent principal overhedging. Also, the contractual term of a derivative and its underlying loan should be judged in advance.
- The third and fourth examples are the least grave. If a firm has made the best estimate in advance, unforeseen market changes must be accepted.

3. Interest payable remains variable with derivatives

The third category of derivatives blunders is affected by the fact that interest payable remains variable with derivatives. A loan has a fixed or a variable interest rate. In the case of a fixed interest rate there is absolute certainty about the interest payable over the full term of the loan. In the case of a variable interest rate, certainty in interest payable can partly be created by using a derivative. The crux is in the word *partly*. This is due to the fact that interest payable consists of three elements which cannot all be fixed:

Elements of variable interest payable

	Reference rate
+	Markup
+	Liquidity premium
	Interest payable

The basis is a reference rate, like Euribor or LIBOR, or a bank's derivative of the money market rate. On top of the reference rate, a firm pays a ***markup*** that is firm specific and depends on the credit risk assessment of the firm by the bank. Furthermore, a ***liquidity premium*** can be added by the bank.

When a variable loan is fixed with a derivative, such as with an interest rate swap, only the reference rate is fixed. The markup and possibly the liquidity premium are not fixed. Consequently, using an interest rate swap does not fix interest payable.

In the case of a fixed interest rate loan, all three elements are locked in. Table 1.2 provides an overview of the three elements of interest payable on a fixed loan and on a variable loan with an interest rate swap.

Table 1.2 **The three elements of interest payable**

Interest payable elements	Fixed rate loan	Variable loan with interest rate swap
Reference rate	Fixed	Fixed
Markup	Fixed	Variable
Liquidity premium	Fixed	Fixed or variable
Interest payable	**Fixed**	**Variable**

Example **Interest payable remains variable with derivatives**

A manufacturing firm wants to construct a new production facility. The firm wants to be certain about the interest payable over the full term of the loan. The firm receives two loan proposals form its bank: one with fixed interest and one with variable interest in combination with an interest rate swap. The firm opts for the latter alternative because interest payable is lower compared to the fixed loan.

Several years later the economy weakens and the firm's results suffer. The firm receives a notice from the bank: due to the deteriorated financials and consequent higher risk profile, the bank has negatively adjusted the credit risk profile of the firm. Accordingly, the lower credit rating leads to a higher markup and interest payable increases.

Key issues of derivatives blunders

Interest payable remains variable with derivatives

Due to the fact that many loan agreements allow markup adjustments, especially in financial and economic crises, not fully understanding which part of interest payable is fixed is a common derivatives blunder.

4. Negative value of derivatives

The fourth category of derivatives blunders relates to the negative value of derivatives. Derivatives have a market value. Due to transaction costs the market value is (slightly) negative at inception. During the life of the derivative the market value fluctuates and may be positive, negative or zero.

If the firm wishes to sell the derivative during its life, this can have serious consequences if the market value is negative. There are three main negative scenarios:

1. The owner of the firm wants to sell the firm or discontinue its activities.
2. The firm repays the underlying loan early (partially).
3. The bank runs higher risk on the firm.

1. The owner of the firm wants to sell the firm or discontinue its activities

In this case the market value of the derivatives has to be settled between the firm and the bank. In the case of adverse market interest rate movements, this can potentially be a large sum. The firm needs to be able to generate sufficient cash to pay the bank. This may cause a problem.

Example

The owner of the firm wants to sell the firm or discontinue its activities

An SME business has long ago signed a variable loan agreement in combination with an interest rate swap. Interest rates have since fallen. The business owner sells his business. He receives a settlement notice from his bank instructing him to pay the negative market value of the interest rate swap.

This is an issue business owners do not always consider when entering into an interest rate swap agreement. Nevertheless, in the case of a fixed rate loan, settlement with the bank would also be due.

If market interest rates had increased instead of decreased, the picture would be different. In the case of a variable rate loan in combination with an interest rate swap, the derivative would have a positive value. The business owner would receive cash from his bank. In contrast, in the case of a fixed rate loan, the firm would receive no compensation.

2. The firm repays the underlying loan early (partially)

In the case of an interest rate swap an open position arises if a firm engages in early partial or full repayment. In order to close the open position the positive or negative value of the open part will have to be settled.

Example

The firm repays the underlying loan early (partially)

The cash flow of a small sized firm exceeds expectations. In order to reduce interest payments, management decides on early repayment of half of the principal of the variable rate loan. The firm receives a note from its bank indicating that the principal of the interest rate swap should also be halved in order to avoid an open derivatives position. Due to significantly lower market interest rates, a considerable negative market value must be paid by the firm.

---

3. The bank runs higher risk on the firm

If the negative market value of a firm's derivative increases, this increases the risk of the bank on the firm, the reason being that if the firm becomes bankrupt, there may not be enough money left to settle the negative market value. In order to mitigate this risk, banks usually work out, with margin calls or with a financing commitment, the maximum amount at risk with a customer. With margin calls the negative value is placed on deposit in cash or in cash equivalence. With a financing commitment the bank monitors that all the firm's obligations with counterparty risk are within the maximum commitment. When the negative market value of a derivative increases, it decreases the room available under the financing commitment. As a result the liquidity available to the firm decreases.

Example

The bank runs higher risk on the firm

A trade firm has a working capital facility with its bank in combination with an interest rate swap. The negative value of the interest rate swap increases. The bank deducts the negative market value of the interest swap from the total commitment to the firm, which is at that point unknown to the firm (sometimes banks make their commitment explicit to their customers and sometimes they don't). To its delight the trade firm receives a large order from a customer. In order to purchase the goods, the firm needs cash and draws under its working capital facility. The necessary cash is within the limit of the working capital facility. However, the bank indicates that due to the higher negative value of the derivative a portion of the credit limit is blocked. As a result less cash can be drawn. This leads to a liquidity problem for the firm.

Key issues of derivatives blunders

Negative value of derivatives

Through different mechanisms, the negative market value of derivatives can have strong effects on the liquidity of the firm. It is vital that firms understand these mechanisms before entering into derivative contracts.

5. Link between derivative and underlying loan

The fifth category of derivatives blunders is concerned with the link between the derivative and the underlying loan. If a firm has a variable rate loan and an interest rate swap and wants or needs to lend from another bank, it will have to repay its debt at its old bank with the cash from the new bank's loan. Depending on the details of the swap contract, the value of the interest rate swap will have to be settled between the firm and the old bank. Depending on the market value of the interest rate swap, this can be a positive or a negative cash flow.

Example

Firm wants to leave bank

A small sized firm believes it is better served at another bank and has received a satisfactory loan agreement from the new bank. Based on the meagre results of the firm, the new bank is just able ▶

to match the principal of the loan at its current bank. The firm intends to repay the variable rate loan at the current bank with the proceeds of the loan from the new bank. The firm receives a settlement notice from its current bank requesting payment of the negative market value of the interest rate swap. Now a problem arises: the firm does not have the cash available to pay the negative market value, nor is there room for a higher loan at the new bank.

Example

Bank wants firm to leave

A medium sized firm has a variable rate term loan and an interest rate swap. The economy is fragile and the firm's performance is weak. Due to a change in the bank's strategy, its focus is now on large firms. Therefore, the medium sized firm is asked to leave the bank and to repay its debt and negative value of the interest rate swap. This causes a problem: is another bank willing to refinance both the debt and the negative value of the derivative?

Key issues of derivatives blunders

If a firm's derivative is linked to an underlying bank loan, this is potentially hazardous for both parties as it can create an unwanted interdependency.

Part 2

UNDERSTANDING THE FIRM'S EXPOSURE TO INTEREST RATE RISK

INTRODUCTION TO PART 2

Part 2 will help you understand how a firm is exposed to interest rate risk. We will investigate this and will specifically examine the key source of exposure for the firm: bank financing.

Part 1 showed you how not to do it. Part 2 represents the first out of four stages to show you how it is done. In the natural sequence of a firm's interest rate risk management process, analysing a firm's sources of exposure to interest rate risk is the first stage. The subsequent stages are discussed in Parts 3, 4 and 5.

I'll first discuss the four sources of a firm's exposure to interest rate risk. Despite the fact that in practice firms generally focus on hedging long-term loans, I want you to be aware of all possible sources of exposure. As bank financing is the primary source of exposure, we'll then explore the core types of bank financing and examine some of its most important aspects with respect to interest rate risk.

2

Four sources of exposure to interest rate risk

INTRODUCTION

It is obvious that without exposure to interest rates there will be no interest rate risk. There are two conditions for a firm to be exposed to interest rate risk. First, the firm needs to have interest-bearing assets or liabilities. Second, the interest rate related to the source of exposure needs to be variable.

Regarding the first condition for exposure to interest rate risk, we'll discuss the four possible interest-bearing assets and liabilities that a firm can have: long-term loans, short-term loans, cash and cash equivalents and financial non-current assets. With respect to the second condition for interest rate risk, the interest rate that is related to a specific exposure can be either fixed or variable, or can be variable now and fixed in the future or vice versa.

Basically all firms are exposed to interest rate risk due to the fact that they are either short of funds and need to borrow money or they have excess funds and deposit money. When borrowing money, a firm has to pay interest on the principal of the loan. When lending money, a firm receives interest payments. Therefore, these are called interest-bearing positions.

These borrowing or lending activities are shown in the financial statements of a firm. The principals of loans are represented on the asset or liability side of the balance sheet. The interest payable or receivable is represented in the income statement and the cash flow statement.

A firm is exposed to interest rate risk under two conditions:

1. It has current or future interest-bearing assets or liabilities.
2. The interest is variable now or in the future.

CURRENT OR FUTURE INTEREST-BEARING ASSETS OR LIABILITIES

Interest-bearing positions can be divided according to their moment of existence into:

- Current interest-bearing positions
- Future interest-bearing positions

Current interest-bearing positions

Current interest-bearing positions are in the balance sheet. Here you will find the current exposures at balance sheet date (usually as at year-end). These exposures are therefore a snapshot in time: the information is already out of date for the reader. The balance sheet only tells you the principal of the interest-bearing positions. Information on debt repayment schedules and the amount of interest due can often be found in the notes to the financial statements.

Figure 2.1

Balance sheet

Assets	Liabilities
Intangible non-current assets	Equity:
Property, plant and equipment	Share capital
Financial non-current assets	Reserves
Total non-current assets	**Total equity**
Inventory	Provisions
Receivables	Long-term loans
Cash and cash equivalents	Short-term loans
Total current assets	**Total current liabilities**
Total assets	**Total liabilities**

The balance sheet provides you with information on the four sources of interest rate risk (they are highlighted):

- Long-term loans
- Short-term loans
- Cash and cash equivalents
- Financial non-current assets

Long-term loans

Long-term loans are loans with a remaining term of more than one year. All items in the balance sheet under long-term loan capital are in principle interest-bearing.

Short-term loans

Short-term loans, which are part of current liabilities, are loans with a term of less than one year. Current liabilities may include both interest-bearing and non-interest-bearing positions. Examples of non-interest-bearing current liabilities are creditors, tax payable and prepayments.

Cash and cash equivalents

A cash balance in the current account usually generates little or no interest. Firms however want to maximise the interest they receive on their cash. For this reason, cash is placed in the money market, either in time deposits or other money market products. Therefore, particularly if substantial sums are involved cash will be interest-bearing.

The cash position can be used for repaying interest-bearing positions on the liability side of the balance sheet. It is therefore advisable to calculate a firm's net debt position by subtracting the cash balance from total interest-bearing liabilities.

Financial non-current assets

Financial non-current assets include loans to third parties for which interest is received. These are therefore interest-bearing positions. Note: financial non-current assets may also include participating interests in other firms. Participating interests in other firms are not interest-bearing.

Future interest-bearing positions

The balance sheet provides information about interest rate exposure in the past. For future interest rate exposure, you depend on a firm's forecast of the four interest-bearing positions. Is a refinancing upcoming? Are there plans for a new building? Is financing going to be repaid early?

All interest from interest-bearing positions is accounted for in the interest line of the income statement. Usually the income statement is presented as follows (the interest line item is highlighted):

Revenue
\- Procurement costs
= Gross margin
\- Other expenses
= EBITDA
\- Depreciation
\- Amortisation of goodwill
= EBIT
\- Interest
= EBT
\- Tax
= Net profit

Warning: other interest in the income statement

The interest paid on long- and short-term loans and the interest received on cash and cash equivalents and financial non-current assets should more or less add up to the interest amount in the interest line in the income statement. There are three complicating factors. First, there may be interest in the interest line from sources that are not represented in the balance sheet, such as interest costs in leasing payments. Second, the interest line can also include accounting items other than interest paid or received, such as foreign exchange premiums and discounts or issue costs of loans. Third, there might be interest costs in other line items in the income statement, for example a construction company can accrue interest costs on projects under procurement costs.

VARIABLE INTEREST RATE NOW OR IN THE FUTURE

I can be brief about variable interest rates: if the interest rate is fixed for any reason whatsoever, a firm has no interest rate exposure because interest due in the future is certain upfront. If the interest is variable, the future interest payable or receivable is uncertain and the firm has interest rate risk.

A firm can have a variable interest rate for several reasons. These could include:

- It has a working capital facility based on a variable rate.
- It will sign a new variable interest rate mortgage soon.
- It has a long-term loan based on a variable rate that has been fixed with an interest rate swap for half the term of the loan. The interest rate swap reaches maturity soon.

3

Bank financing as primary source of exposure

INTRODUCTION

In the previous chapter we discussed the sources of exposure to interest rate risk. Of the four sources of exposure, most firms are exposed to interest rate risk through short- and long-term loans from banks. In this chapter I'll focus on three types of bank financing: current account overdraft, medium-term loans and long-term loans. Furthermore, I'll examine three aspects of bank financing that influence interest rate risk: collateral, repayment methods and pricing.

From the point of view of the term of bank financing, a current account overdraft 'officially' has the shortest term as it is cancellable daily by either party. Nevertheless, a current account overdraft may exist for a long time if it is not terminated. Furthermore, as a current account overdraft is used to finance working capital, the interest payable by the firm is volatile as the daily balance will fluctuate and the credit conditions may be changed by the bank. The daily cancellability of a current account overdraft has to be taken into account when considering hedging interest rate risk as its term is unpredictable.

In comparison to a current account overdraft, medium- and long-term loans have a fixed term. Where medium-term loans are mainly used to finance property, plant and equipment (PPE) investments or to consolidate the permanent part of a current account overdraft or inventory, long-term loans are usually used to finance long-term assets, such as real estate. Even though most parameters of medium- and long-term loan agreements are fixed in advance, uncertainty remains with respect to variable interest rates, variability in markup and a possible breach of (financial) covenants.

Collateral provided by the borrower reduces the risk for the bank. As a consequence, the higher the collateral value the lower the markup. Furthermore, the more easily the collateral of the firm can be transformed into cash, the higher its collateral value. Ultimately however the provision of collateral is decided by the relative negotiating powers of the firm and the bank.

There are different debt repayment methods and repayment features that can be tailored to the firm's financial situation. First and foremost the projected cash flows of the firm should be sufficient to cover the interest and debt redemption payment obligations over the full term of the loan.

Regarding the price of money, a bank charges both interest and fees. Some of these are fixed and others are variable. Some are paid upfront and others during the term of the credit. We'll discuss the three elements of interest and three common types of fees: facility fee, closing costs and commitment fee.

CURRENT ACCOUNT OVERDRAFT

The first type of bank financing is the current account overdraft. Many firms use a current account overdraft for financing current assets such as inventory and receivables. An important feature is its daily cancellability, which raises questions regarding the hedging horizon if interest rate risk is mitigated. We'll discuss this issue and other important characteristics of the current account overdraft, such as the overdraft limit, advance financing and interest volatility.

The current account overdraft originates from the oldest activity of commercial banking: the funding of commodity transactions. In these transactions, there is a funding requirement at the moment firms have to pay their supplier for the goods they have received. Once the buyer has paid for the goods, the financing requirement disappears: therefore this type of transaction is self-liquidating. The firm can meet this cash requirement either by holding a cash balance or by arranging a current account overdraft facility.

In principle most firms have to cope with the timing difference between cash receipts and expenses. However, there are exceptions. For example, publishers who receive payments from subscribers before the product is delivered. Such firms may have a negative net working capital: they are financed by their customers!

Overdraft limit

A firm will strive to keep its current account balance to a minimum because cash generates little return. If a firm has a current account overdraft facility, it can get by with a lower cash balance. An overdraft limit is agreed between the bank and the borrower in advance. Exceeding this limit is in principle not permitted and if it does occur penalty interest is due. The level of the overdraft limit depends on the annual turnover that flows through the current account.

A current account overdraft is mainly used for absorbing fluctuations in cash as a result of payments and receipts, i.e. to fund short-term cash requirements due to movements in the firm's inventory, debtors and creditors.

Advance financing

For smaller firms, the maximum debit balance permitted within the agreed limit is determined on the basis of the advance funding of debtors and inventory. For instance, advance funding of the debtor portfolio of up to 70% and of inventory of up to 40% may be agreed. Usually, smaller firms will regularly provide the bank with a list of receivables which will be pledged to the bank.

Daily callable

An important feature of a current account overdraft is that it can be cancelled on a daily basis either by the firm or by the bank. If the bank cancels the overdraft, if there is a debit balance it has to be repaid immediately. In practice however, after notifying the firm of the cancellation, the bank will give the firm a reasonable period of time to repay the debt. The fact that the overdraft can be cancelled with only one day's notice implies that the conditions under which the credit is granted – the limit, the collateral and the debit interest – can be changed by the bank at all times.

Further, because it can be cancelled daily, a current account overdraft is in principle not suitable for financing non-current assets. If the bank calls in the overdraft facility, the firm could be forced to sell its machinery, possibly threatening its continuity. An overdraft facility is therefore primarily intended to finance current assets that can be liquidated fairly quickly if necessary. Nevertheless, the short-term nature does not exclude the possibility that a current account overdraft may exist for a longer period of time.

Interest

A firm pays interest on the number of days for which its current account is actually in debit and receives interest on the same terms (debit balance x debit interest and/or credit balance x credit interest). Normally, the credit interest on a current account is zero or very low. You have to be aware that the interest amount is volatile as the daily balance will fluctuate. Also, credit conditions may be changed by the bank at any time.

When considering hedging interest rate risk arising from a current account overdraft you have to take account of the volatility of the interest amount and of the daily cancellability as it leads to uncertainty regarding the level of exposure to hedge and the term of the hedge. Overhedging is a realistic risk: see the derivatives blunders on overhedging in Part 1.

MEDIUM- AND LONG-TERM LOANS

The second and third types of bank financing are respectively medium-term loans and long-term loans. Medium- and long-term loans are the most common sources of exposure to interest rate risk that firms hedge with derivatives. Most parameters of medium- and long-term loans are fixed before entering into the financing agreement. Nevertheless, uncertainty remains with respect to variable interest rates, variability in markup and a possible breach of (financial) covenants. We'll discuss how firms use medium- and long-term loans, how the term of these loans is established, common loan features and the conditions for calling in the loan by banks.

Use of medium- and long-term loans

The features of medium-term and long-term loans are very much alike. Nevertheless, firms use them for different reasons. Medium-term loans are usually used for three purposes:

1. Replacement investments

These investments are made to replace existing PPE. Examples are machinery at an industrial firm or motor vehicles at a transport firm.

2. Expansion investments

Expansion investments also relate to PPE. However, unlike replacement investments, expansion investments result from a growth in demand. For example, a transport firm orders additional vehicles to meet an increase in demand for its freight services.

3. Consolidation

Medium-term loans can also be used if a firm wishes to consolidate its debt – in other words, if a firm wishes to convert part of its current liabilities into longer-term loans. Consolidation usually consists of converting the permanent element of inventory and accounts receivable, financed by a current account overdraft, into a medium-term loan.

Medium-term loans are therefore mainly appropriate for the funding of PPE and the permanent element of inventory and accounts receivable. Like medium-term loans, long-term loans can also be used to fund PPE investments. Mortgages are provided with the underlying property as collateral.

Loan term

Regarding the most suitable term for PPE investments, two factors are important:

1. Depreciation term

The term of a medium- or long-term loan should not be longer than the depreciation term of the PPE investment. If a longer term is taken, there is uncertainty that the PPE investment will pay for itself over the depreciation period. In this case, either the PPE investment is being written off too quickly or this is a loss-making investment. Both situations are undesirable.

2. Repayment capacity

The question is whether the firm can repay the loan within the depreciation term of the PPE investment. An assessment of the firm's debt repayment capacity after the investment has to be made. With regard to the optimal term for financing the permanent elements of inventory and accounts receivable, since there is no depreciation, the maturities of a term loan and the debt redemption schedule are usually based on the firm's estimated future repayment capability.

The upper limit for the term of a medium- or long-term loan is therefore determined by the useful life of the PPE investment. The lower limit is determined by the firm's debt repayment capacity.

Loan features

The principal is provided either in a lump sum or in instalments. Repayment is according to a previously agreed repayment schedule. Other features are:

- Amounts repaid can usually not be drawn down again. However, in the case of a roll-over loan, a type of medium-term loan, the borrower can continue to draw up to the limit.
- The loan has a fixed term and unlike a current account overdraft cannot be cancelled on a daily basis. In case of cancellation break-up costs can be due.

Conditions for calling in

A medium- or long-term loan can be called in by the loan provider if the payment of interest or debt redemption are not made in due time. A loan can also be called in if (financial) covenants in the loan agreement are breached.

COLLATERAL

The first important aspect of bank financing with respect to interest rate risk is collateral because it reduces credit risk for the lender and therefore can reduce interest payable by the borrower resulting from a lower markup. The more easily the collateral can be transformed into cash, the higher the collateral value. Collateral is part of the negotiations on the price of a loan between the firm and the bank. We'll discuss how the collateral value is determined.

The estimated collateral value is based on the expected proceeds at execution. The calculated value can be set against a firm's credit facilities. If the collateral value is higher than the amount of the credit facilities, the loans are fully collateralised. Otherwise, there is a lack of cover. When calculating the value of collateral, a distinction is made between the three types of collateral:

1. Commercial collateral
2. Personal collateral
3. Intangible collateral

1. Commercial collateral

There are certain guidelines for determining the collateral value of assets. We'll discuss real estate, inventory and non-current assets and debtors.

Real estate

In the case of real estate, the collateral value is usually set at approximately 70% of the estimated execution value provided by an external valuator. The reason for not using the full execution value of the real estate is that the mortgage deed contains various charges that fall under the mortgage entitlement. These mainly concern auction costs and interest arrears. If a bank were to accept the full execution value of real estate, it would in fact be creating a situation of lack of cover. So, if the execution value of real estate is 70% of the value in private sale, the collateral value of real estate is circa 50% of the value in private sale.

Inventory and non-current assets

The guideline for inventory and non-current assets is more difficult to quantify, but a valuation similar to that used for real estate, i.e. 50% of the value in private sale, is normal. The value of the inventory and other assets in private sale can be determined by a recognised broker, but normally the book value of these assets is used as the basic measure for the calculation.

When determining the collateral value, account has to be taken of any creditors that have a preferred status over the bank. For instance, when determining the collateral value of a second mortgage, the claim of the first mortgage provider has to be deducted from the collateral value. The same applies to claims held by leasing companies or creditors. Positive adjustments to the collateral value of inventory can be applied for inventory that can be readily liquidated. Negative adjustments are made if there is a high proportion of semi-finished product or obsolete inventory.

Debtors

For debtors the collateral value is usually set at approximately 60% of the nominal value as long as a list of pledged receivables is provided. An undisclosed pledge of named receivables is only effective if transfer of these receivables via lists of pledged receivables is a regular occurrence. A higher percentage will be used if a firm has insured its accounts receivable with credit insurance or if the debtors are government institutions. A lower percentage will be used if the payment behaviour of the customers falls short of the normal payment terms in the industry sector concerned, or if the customer base contains a relatively high proportion of bad payers.

The total value of the commercial collateral can then be compared to the amount of credit. Any remaining lack of cover can be met by the provision of personal or intangible collateral. This mainly applies to smaller companies.

2. Personal collateral

The value that can be attached to a security or guarantee has to be assessed in each individual case. Requiring a security from directors only has legal significance in the case of a legal entity, in particular a public limited or a private limited firm. For business entities that are natural persons, the owner is automatically personally liable.

If the bank cannot explicitly value a particular element of the collateral, the security is usually termed a moral security and is often included as a memorandum item.

3. Intangible collateral

No collateral value can normally be allocated to intangible collateral. The only exception to this could be a repurchase commitment.

REPAYMENT METHODS

The second important aspect of bank financing regarding interest rate risk is repayment methods as with each loan repayment the principal of the loan is reduced and as a result the firm's exposure to interest rate risk decreases. There are different debt repayment methods and repayment features that can be tailored to the firm's interest and debt repayment obligations. We'll discuss the four basic repayment methods and three common features that are related to debt repayment.

These are the four basic repayment methods for medium- and long-term loans:

1. Linear

Linear repayment is a common method. The same amount of debt is repaid on a regular basis (monthly, quarterly, semi-annually or annually) throughout the term of the loan. Because interest is calculated on the outstanding debt, which is declining, the amount of interest also declines over time (ceteris paribus).

It is characteristic of the linear repayment method that debt service is highest at the start of the loan.

Debt service = interest and debt redemption payments

2. Annuity

In the case of repayment on an annuity basis, debt service is the same throughout the loan's life. At the beginning debt service consists of a higher proportion of interest and a lower proportion of debt repayment. Towards the end of the loan's life, the reverse applies.

3. Balloon

If a firm has limited ability for debt repayment in the early part of the loan's life, balloon debt repayment is an option. Debt redemption is lower at the beginning of the loan and higher towards the end. This gives a firm time to generate the cash flow necessary to make the debt repayments.

4. Bullet

In the case of a bullet loan, the principal of the loan does not change during its life. The loan is repaid in full as a lump sum at maturity.

Next to these four repayment methods, there are three common features that relate to the repayment of loans:

Grace period

In most cases debt redemption starts from the beginning of a loan. A repayment-free period may however be agreed, known as a grace period. Repayment is postponed until after the end of the grace period.

Debt sculpting

Tailor-made debt redemption schedules can be arranged. The repayment schedule is aligned with the firm's projected cash flows so that it will most likely be able to meet its debt service.

Early repayment

A chosen debt redemption schedule is determined upfront for the entire life of the loan. It may however be the case that a firm wishes to repay all or part of a loan before maturity. The loan provider is then entitled to charge break-up costs.

PRICING

The third important aspect of bank financing relating to interest rate risk is pricing. This is because it constitutes all costs, consisting of interest and fees, that a firm has to pay for borrowing money from a bank. These are recognised as interest expenses in the interest line item in the income statement and the cash flow statement.

The pricing element in loan agreements has two forms:

1. Interest
2. Fees

1. Interest

The interest payable on a loan consists of three elements: (i) funding costs, (ii) a profit margin and (iii) a firm-specific risk markup. The higher the estimated risk that the firm will not be able to meet its debt service obligations, the higher the risk markup. The higher the level of cover provided by collateral, the lower the risk markup.

2. Fees

Fees can be seen as payment for the services provided by the bank in the lending process. The most common fees are:

Facility fee

The facility fee is charged when a bank makes a credit facility available for a previously agreed period. The facility fee is calculated periodically on the average debit balance, the highest debit balance or the overdraft limit.

Closing costs

Closing costs are a one-off payment calculated over the principal sum of the facility provided. Closing costs are charged when the loan is signed.

Commitment fee

A commitment fee is paid for the costs of the reserves a bank has to hold for an overdraft. The reason is that the unused part of the overdraft can be drawn by a firm at once and in full. To ensure this can occur without problems, a bank has to retain a reserve. The costs of holding this reserve are charged to the firm in the form of a commitment fee. This fee is calculated periodically over the unused portion of the credit facility.

Part 3

MEASURING THE IMPACT OF INTEREST RATE RISK ON THE FIRM

INTRODUCTION TO PART 3

Core to Part 3 is measuring the impact of interest rate movements on the financial statements of the firm. In order to examine these effects, we first have to understand the workings of the financial markets where the fluctuations of the variable interest rate originate.

Part 3 is the second out of four stages in a firm's interest rate risk management process. It builds on the sources of exposure to interest rate risk examined in Part 2.

I'll discuss the workings of the financial markets as they determine the firm's interest payable and receivable. Then, I'll examine the impact of movements in the firm's interest payable and receivable on its financial statements. The financial markets, consisting of the money markets and the capital markets, are also related to the interest rate derivatives examined in Part 5 because they are all affected by money market rate changes and some by capital market rate movements. Measuring the impact on the firm's financial statements by interest rate movements in the financial markets is important because it is a key reason for firms to hedge interest rate risk and as such an important building block for the analytical method presented in Part 6.

4

The financial markets

INTRODUCTION

The reason for investigating the financial markets is twofold. First, the variable interest rates that firms receive or pay on respectively interest-bearing assets or liabilities (discussed in Chapters 2 and 3) are based on the reference rates in the money market (the part of the financial markets for short-term debt), such as Euribor and LIBOR. Second, when firms use interest rate derivatives such as swaps, FRAs or caps, floors, collars and swaptions to mitigate interest rate risk, these derivatives are related to specific money market reference rates. The capital market, which is the part of the financial markets for longer-term debt, is discussed because derivatives such as swaps and swaptions are related to the rates in this market. Interest rate derivatives are discussed in depth in Part 5.

I'll start by discussing the yield curve because this curve represents the prices in the financial markets for debt for different terms. Then I'll examine how the prices are established on the shorter term (money market) and the longer term (capital market). As firms that are exposed to interest rate risk are exposed to money market movements, we'll spend most time discussing those.

THE YIELD CURVE

The yield curve, also called the term structure of interest rates, depicts the relationship between market interest rates (yield) and differences in the term for debt securities of the same credit quality. It is a line that connects the interest rates for different maturities between one day to around 30 years. There are different yield curves for different kinds of debt, for instance for government bonds of different countries, and for debt with different currencies and credit risk.

There are three types of yield curves. First, the swap curve. This is the yield curve for debt valued at its nominal value. Second, the zero coupon yield curve. This yield curve represents debt without coupon and with only one cash flow at maturity. It is often used for discounting cash flows. Third, the forward yield curve. This yield curve represents future rates calculated on the basis of the current rates.

The three basic shapes of yield curves

Depending on market circumstances, the yield curve can take several shapes. There are three basic forms:

- Normal yield curve
- Inverted yield curve
- Flat yield curve

The normal yield curve

This is the most prevalent shape of the yield curve. In a normal yield curve short-term debt has lower yield than long-term debt. As a result the yield curve has an upward slope. The graph in Figure 4.1 shows a normal yield curve.

Figure 4.1

The normal yield curve

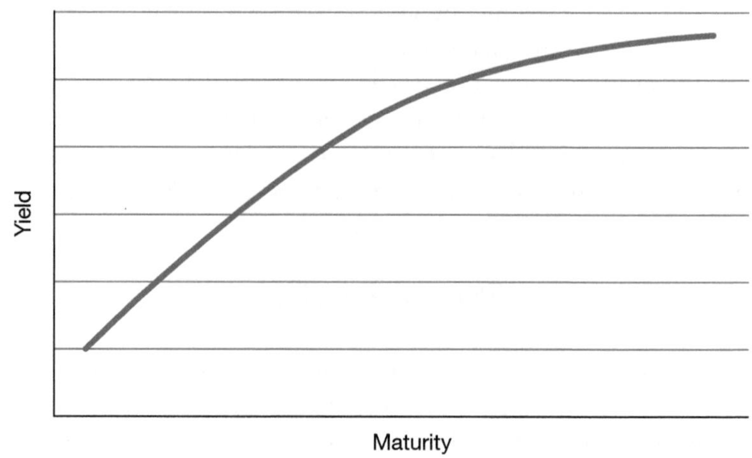

The rationale behind the normal yield curve is that investors require a higher return when money is invested for a longer period. This is because the chance that the debtor goes bankrupt is higher in the longer term and investors require more compensation for higher risk. Also, inflation may increase. Finally, an investor wants to be compensated when his money is invested over a longer period of time as he is unable to use it in other ways.

The inverted yield curve

The yield curve is inverted in a case where short-term interest rates are higher than long-term interest rates. The graph in Figure 4.2

shows an inverted yield curve. Generally a yield curve does not stay inverted for long.

Figure 4.2

The inverted yield curve

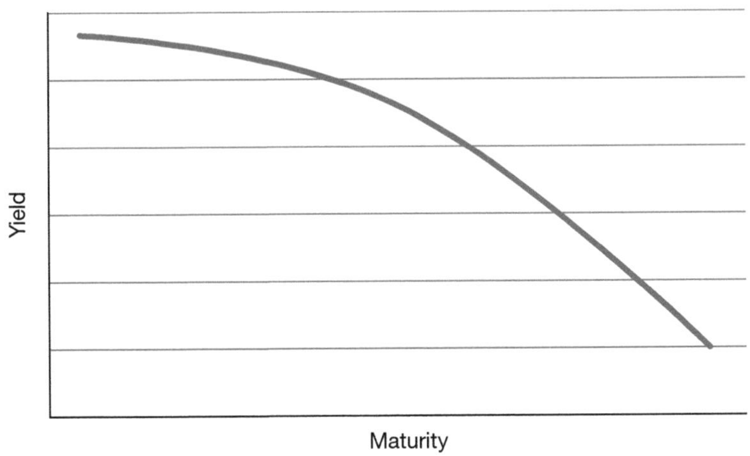

The most important reasons for an inverse yield curve are an increase of the interest rate by central banks and/or an expected decrease of inflation over time. Another reason may be that parties are not willing to lend money to each other, such as during a credit crisis. In such a case the demand for short-term debt increases strongly and short-term rates will increase.

The flat yield curve

A flat yield curve implies that short- and long-term interest rates are more or less the same. The graph in Figure 4.3 illustrates a flat yield curve.

Figure 4.3

The flat yield curve

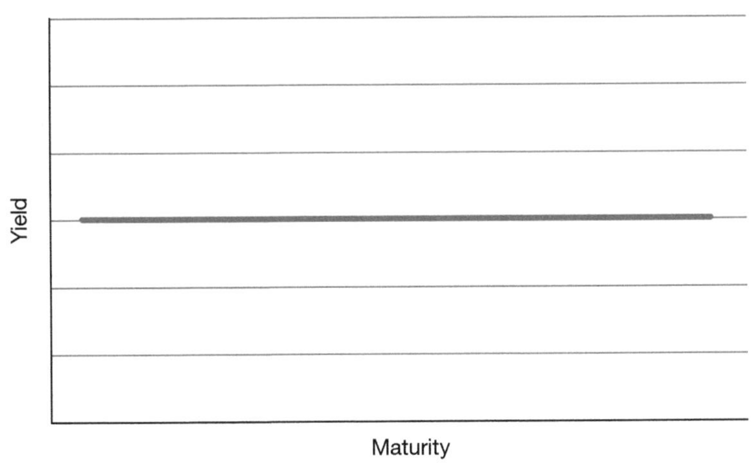

A flat yield curve is unusual and exists in the case where a normal yield curve turns into an inverted yield curve or vice versa.

Yield curve theory

There are three main theories that attempt to explain the shape of the yield curve:

- Market expectations theory
- Liquidity preference theory
- Market segmentation theory

Market expectations theory

According to the market expectations theory, the yield curve is only influenced by investors' expectations of the future interest rates. A steep yield curve indicates that the market expects higher interest rates in the future and vice versa.

Liquidity preference theory

According to the liquidity preference theory, the yield curve is not only determined by interest rate expectations, but a liquidity premium for longer-term investments should also be taken into account.

The liquidity premium is a term premium. As with long-term investments investors are exposed to larger risks – for instance with respect to future inflation and having their money tied up for a longer period – and are compensated for this. The longer the term of a loan, the higher the uncertainty and the higher the term premium. Because of the term premium, long-term investments' yields are higher than those of short-term investments and as a result the yield curve slopes upward.

Market segmentation theory

According to the market segmentation theory, investors have a clear preference for a certain term and they require a premium to invest in maturities outside their preferred term. Consequently, supply and demand in markets for short-term and long-term investments is determined mainly independently. If investors prefer liquidity, they will prefer short-term investments over long-term investments. This drives the yields of short-term investments down, creating a normal yield curve shape.

Based on the term of debt the financial markets consist of:

- The money market
- The capital market

In the money market firms can borrow and lend money with terms between one day and one year. In the capital market firms can conclude transactions for longer terms.

THE MONEY MARKET

Only very large parties, such as banks, governments, institutional investors and very large firms have direct access to the money market. The money market, however, is basically an interbank market. The prices that banks charge each other are called interbank prices. A bank will indicate a bid and ask price: it will be interested in borrowing money at the lower bid rate and interested in lending money at the higher offer rate.

Central banks

Central banks play an important role in the money market. The policy of most central banks is directed towards controlling inflation. Two central banks with worldwide importance are:

- European Central Bank (ECB)
- Federal Reserve (FED)

ECB

The ECB is the central bank for Europe's single currency: the euro. The national central banks together with the ECB constitute the Eurosystem, the central banking system of the euro area, which is one of the world's largest currency areas. The euro area comprises 18 European Union countries that have introduced the euro since 1999.[1] The main objective of the ECB is to maintain price stability in the euro area, safeguarding the value of the euro.

The ECB has different instruments to control short-term interest rates. An important instrument is the main refinancing rate. The graph in Figure 4.4 shows the development of the refinancing rate since the introduction of the euro.[2]

FED

The FED is the central bank of the United States. The FED is an independent government institution that is owned by a number

Figure 4.4

ECB refinancing rate (%)

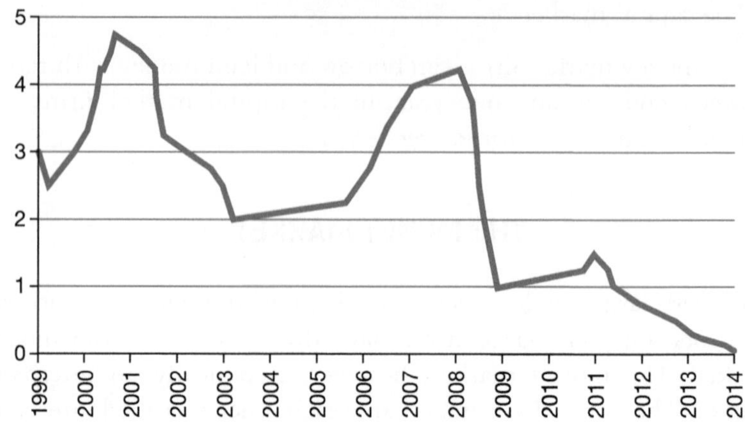

of large banks and not by the state. There are also 12 regional reserve banks. Five members of the regional reserve banks and the seven members of the board of governors of the FED form the Federal Open Market Committee (FOMC). The primary responsibility of the FOMC is to supervise open market operations through monetary policy.

The federal funds rate is the interest rate that banks charge one another for overnight lending. The FED influences the federal funds rate by adding or withdrawing the money supply in order to reach the federal funds target rate. The graph in Figure 4.5 shows the federal funds target rate.[3]

Figure 4.5

Fed funds rate (%)

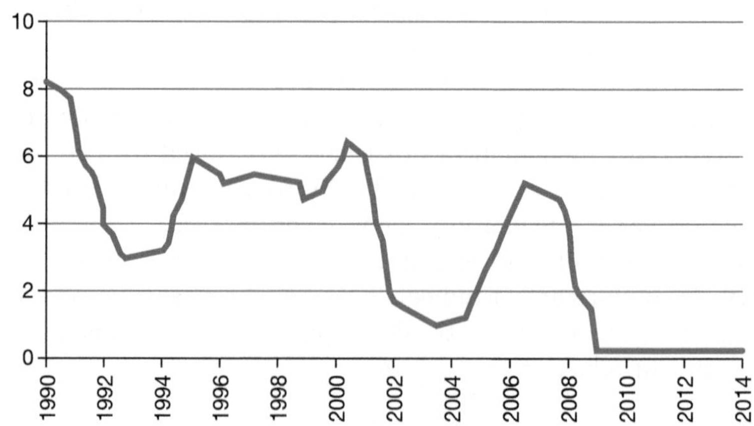

Table 4.1 shows the interest rates of other central banks around the world.[4]

Interest rates of central banks around the world **Table 4.1**

Interest rate	Country	Current rate	Direction	Previous rate	Last change
American (FED)	United States	0.25%	▼	1.00%	12–16–2008
Australian (RBA)	Australia	2.50%	▼	2.75%	08–06–2013
Banco Central	Chile	3.25%	▼	3.50%	09–11–2014
Bank of Korea	South Korea	2.25%	▼	2.50%	08–14–2014
Brazilian (BACEN)	Brazil	11.00%	▲	10.75%	04–02–2014
British (BoE)	Great Britain	0.50%	▼	1.00%	03–05–2009
Canadian (BOC)	Canada	1.00%	▲	0.75%	09–08–2010
Chinese (PBC)	China	6.00%	▼	6.31%	07–06–2012
Czech (CNB)	Czech Republic	0.05%	▼	0.25%	11–01–2012
Danish (Nationalbanken)	Denmark	0.20%	▼	0.30%	05–02–2013
European (ECB)	Europe	0.05%	▼	0.15%	09–04–2014
Hungarian	Hungary	2.10%	▼	2.30%	07–22–2014
Indian (RBI)	India	8.00%	▲	7.75%	01–28–2014
Indonesian (BI)	Indonesia	7.50%	▲	7.25%	11–12–2013
Israeli (BOI)	Israel	0.25%	▼	0.50%	08–25–2014
Japanese (BoJ)	Japan	0.10%	▼	0.10%	10–05–2010
Mexican (Banxico)	Mexico	3.00%	▼	3.50%	06–06–2014
New Zealand	New Zealand	3.50%	▲	3.25%	07–24–2014
Norwegian	Norway	1.50%	▼	1.75%	03–14–2012
Polish	Poland	2.50%	▼	2.75%	07–03–2013
Russian (CBR)	Russia	8.00%	▲	7.50%	07–25–2014
Saudi Arabian	Saudi Arabia	2.00%	▼	2.50%	01–19–2009
South African (SARB)	South Africa	5.75%	▲	5.50%	07–17–2014
Swedish (Riksbank)	Sweden	0.25%	▼	0.75%	07–03–2014
Swiss (SNB)	Switzerland	0.25%	▼	0.50%	03–12–2009
Turkish (CBRT)	Turkey	8.25%	▼	8.75%	07–18–2014

Money market rates

Two of the world's most important reference rates for short-term interest rates are influenced by the ECB's main refinancing rate and by the FED's fund rate. They are respectively Euribor and LIBOR. The interest rates for other parties, such as for most firms, are derived from these interbank rates. In the case that a firm wants to borrow money, a surcharge is added to the interbank rate. In the case that a firm wants to lend money a discount is calculated.

Euribor

Euribor is short for Euro Interbank Offered Rate. Euribor was created in 1999 with the introduction of the euro. Euribor rates are based on the average interest rates at which a panel of 26 European banks borrow unsecured funds from one another in the euro interbank market.[5] The highest and lowest 15% of the quotes collected are eliminated. The remaining rates are averaged and rounded to three decimal places. Euribor is determined and published around 11 a.m. each day.

As of November 2013 there are 8 different Euribor rates with maturities ranging from one week to one year:

- Euribor – 1 week
- Euribor – 2 weeks
- Euribor – 1 month
- Euribor – 2 months
- Euribor – 3 months
- Euribor – 6 months
- Euribor – 9 months
- Euribor – 12 months

The graph in Figure 4.6 shows a snapshot of the Euribor rates.[6]

Figure 4.6

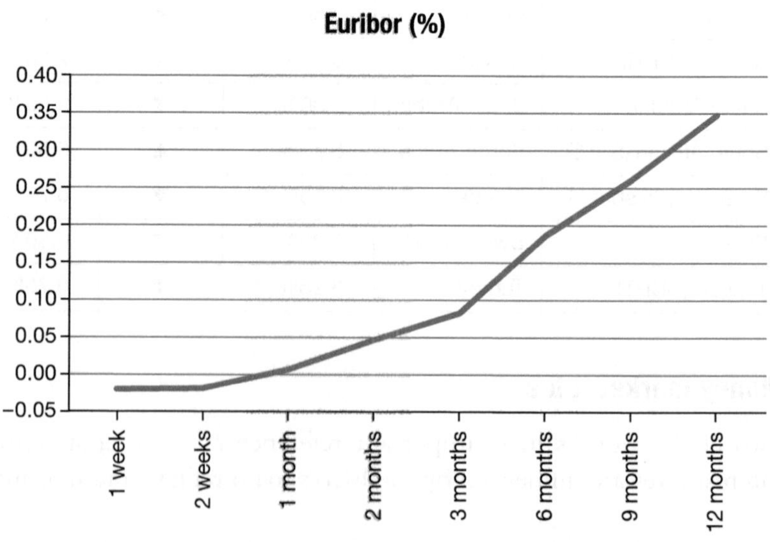

The graph in Figure 4.7 shows 3-months Euribor over time from its inception in 1999.[7]

Figure 4.7

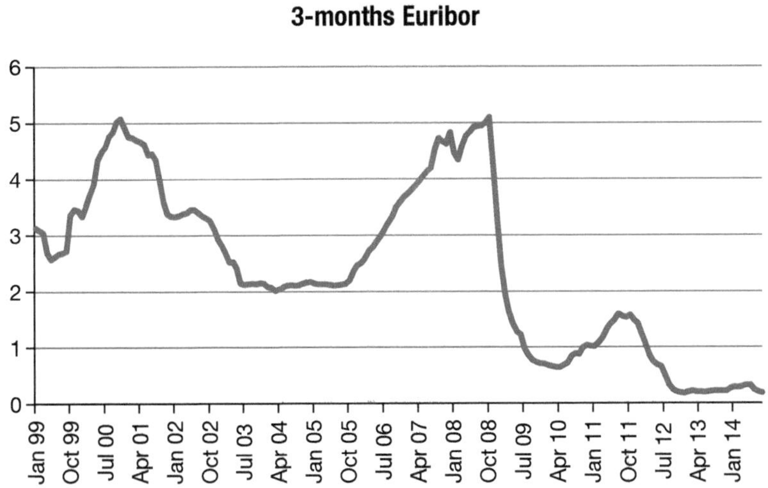

The graph shows the 3-months Euribor rate to be highly volatile within a range of around 0% to 5%. Notice how fast this important reference rate has decreased from slightly above 5% in November 2008 to less than 1.5% only six months later! This means that firms with loans based on 3-months Euribor will have paid 3.5 percentage points less interest in a very short period of time. What happens if the opposite occurs? Are firms that are used to the low interest levels in recent years able to bear the higher interest payments?

LIBOR

LIBOR stands for London Interbank Offered Rate. LIBOR and Euribor are comparable base rates. The main difference is that LIBOR rates are in different currencies. LIBOR reflects the short-term funding costs of major banks active in London. LIBOR is a polled rate which means that a panel of representative banks submits rates which are then combined to give the LIBOR rate. LIBOR is the rate at which the panel banks lend money to one another just prior to 11 a.m. The highest and lowest 25% are removed and the remainder is averaged. LIBOR is published at around 11.45 a.m. (London time). LIBOR is published for five currencies:

- American dollar – USD LIBOR
- British pound sterling – GBP LIBOR

- European euro – EUR LIBOR
- Japanese yen – JPY LIBOR
- Swiss franc – CHF LIBOR

For each currency LIBOR is published in seven maturities:

- 1 day (overnight)
- 1 week
- 1 month
- 2 months
- 3 months
- 6 months
- 12 months

The graph in Figure 4.8 is a snapshot of the LIBOR rates.[8]

Figure 4.8

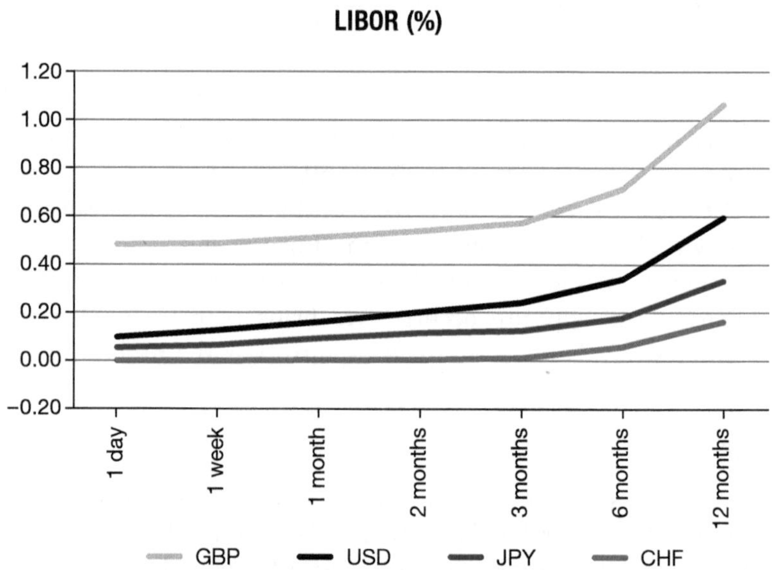

Be aware that the day count convention in the money market for all currencies is 360 days, except for GBP (365 days).

THE CAPITAL MARKET

Interest rates in the capital market are a result of supply and demand and are rarely influenced by central banks. Expected inflation is an important factor determining interest rates. The interest rates in the capital market determine the price of different kinds of debt such as interest on loans for firms or for governments. The most important factors determining the price of debt are: the quality of the debtor, the term of the loan, the chosen interest rate and the liquidity of the debt.

A government can usually borrow at the best conditions as the debtor risk is lowest. The quality of the debtor is based on the probability that he or she will meet their interest and debt redemption obligations. The larger the probability that a debtor will fail to do so, the larger the markup on the riskless interest rate (on government debt). The lower the tradability of debt, the higher the interest payable. Therefore firms that borrow on the OTC-market (a bilateral, tailor-made, transaction between a firm and a bank) pay a higher interest than would have been due on the public market. On the other hand, firms can benefit from the flexibility in principal amount and term provided in the OTC-market.

The graph in Figure 4.9 illustrates the euro and US dollar capital market yield curve.[9]

Figure 4.9

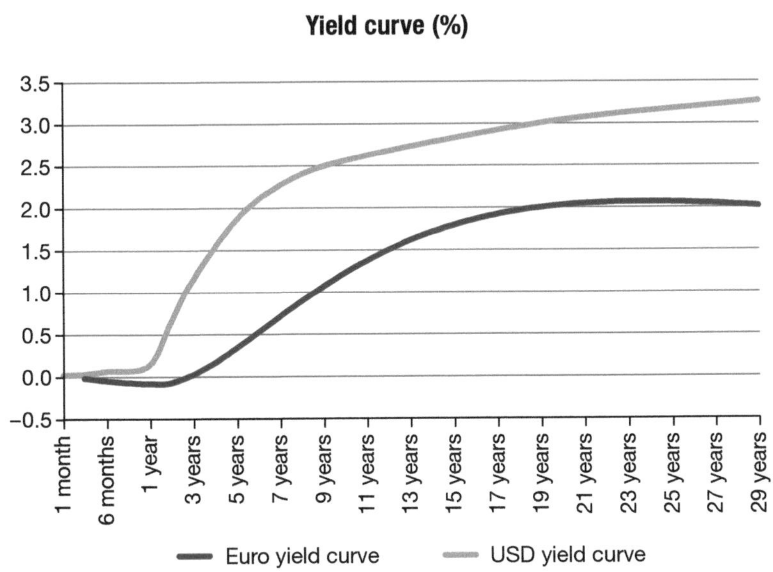

interest rates in the capital market determine the price of different kinds of debt, such as interest on loans for firms or for governments. The most important factors determining the price of debt are: the quality of the debtor, the term of the loan, the chosen interest rate and the liquidity of the debt.

A government can usually borrow at the best conditions as the debtor risk is lowest. The quality of the debtor is based on the probability that he or she will meet their interest and debt redemption obligations. The larger the probability that a debtor will fail to do so, the larger the markup on the riskless interest rate (or government debt). The lower the tradability of debt, the higher the interest payable. Therefore firms that borrow on the OTC market (a bilateral, tailor-made, transaction between a firm and a bank) pay a higher interest than would have been due on the public market. On the other hand, firms can benefit from the flexibility in principal amount and term provided in the OTC market.

The graph in Figure 4.7 illustrates the euro and USD dollar capital market yield curve.

5

Financial statement impact from interest rate movements

INTRODUCTION

In Chapter 4 we've examined how interest rates are determined in the financial markets. In this chapter we'll look at how interest rate movements in the financial markets impact the financial statements of a firm. In order to illustrate the effects we use a central case: Trader. Background information on Trader can be found in Appendix I.

The chapter is quite detailed but the reason for this is because the negative financial impact of interest rate fluctuations is a major risk to the firm. It is outside its sphere of influence and therefore it is often the basis for risk. In particular financial covenants play an important role.

In order to establish the impact of interest rate movements on the firm, we'll discuss six ratios:

1. Liquidity
2. Solvency
3. Financial covenants
4. Cash cycle
5. Profitability
6. Share price ratios

There is a link between each of the six ratios and interest rate risk. I'll explain each of these and then show them in a graph form:

- **Liquidity**: interest payable and receivable influences the cash position of a firm and therewith directly affects liquidity.
- **Solvency**: interest in the income statement passes through to earnings before tax and then to net profit. Ultimately, interest is passed through to retained earnings if it is not distributed in the form of a dividend. As retained earnings are part of equity, and equity is the numerator in the solvency ratio, interest influences the solvency of a firm.
- **Financial covenants**: interest payable and receivable directly influences the ICR, net debt/EBITDA and DSCR ratios and indirectly influences the solvency ratio.
- **Cash cycle**: interest payable and receivable influences the cash position of the firm. Furthermore, the cash and cash equivalents

item in the balance sheet is a source of exposure for interest rate risk.

- **Profitability**: interest payable and receivable influences net profit. Profitability is the relationship between a firm's capital and its profit.
- **Share price ratios**: interest payable and receivable influences three important elements of share price ratios:
  i. net profit
  ii. dividend and
  iii. retained earnings.

In Figures 5.1–5.3, interest and the other elements in the financial statements that are influenced by interest rate risk are highlighted. I also show the links between these elements and the six ratios.

Figure 5.1

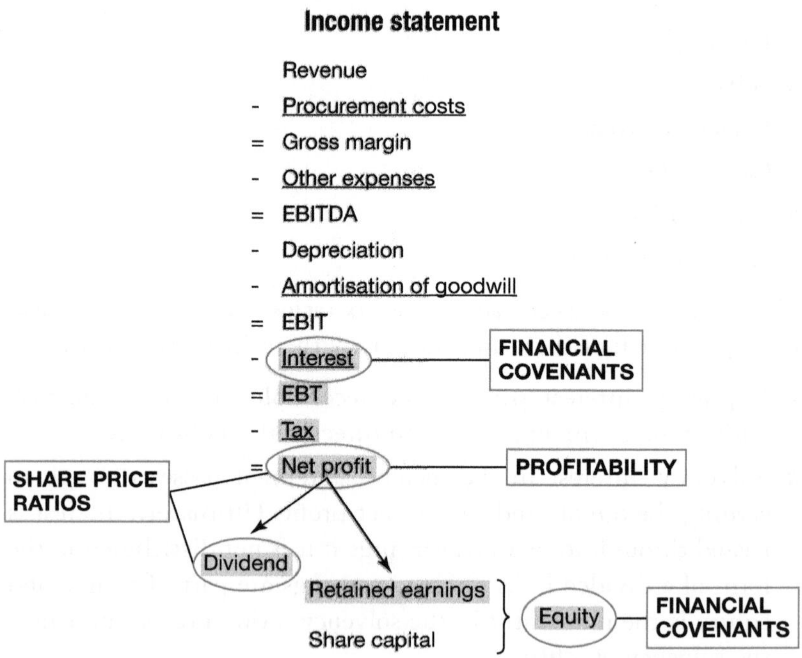

Balance sheet

Figure 5.2

Assets	Liabilities
Intangible non-current assets	Equity:
Property, plant and equipment	Share capital
Financial non-current assets	Reserves
Total non-current assets	**Total equity**
Inventory	Provisions
Receivables	Long-term loans
Cash and cash equivalents	Short-term loans
Total current assets	**Total current liabilities**
Total assets	**Total liabilities**

CASH CYCLE

LIQUIDITY

Cash flow statement

Figure 5.3

Cash at beginning of period
\+ Sales
\- Purchases
\- Salaries
\- Other expenses
\- Investments
\- Acquisitions
\+ Disposals
+/- Issue/repurchase of own shares
\+ New loans and drawdowns of credit
\- Repayments of loans/credits
\+ Repayments of loans/credits granted
\- Provision of loans/credits granted
\+ Grants
\- Tax
\- Dividend paid
\+ Interest received
= **Cash flow available for interest and debt repayment**
\- Interest paid
\- Repayment of loans and credit
= **Interest and debt repayment**
-/-
= Cash at end of period

LIQUIDITY

FINANCIAL COVENANTS

CASH CYCLE

LIQUIDITY

Liquidity is linked to interest rate risk in three ways:

- Interest payments and receipts directly influence the cash position.
- With cash, debt can be repaid, a source of exposure to interest rate risk.
- Cash and cash equivalents are in themselves a source of exposure to interest rate risk.

Liquidity shows the extent to which a firm can meet its payment obligations, such as debt service in the short term (within a year). In extreme cases, a lack of liquidity can endanger a firm's continued existence. It is therefore important that a firm has sufficient liquidity available at all times.

Figure 5.4 **Liquidity**

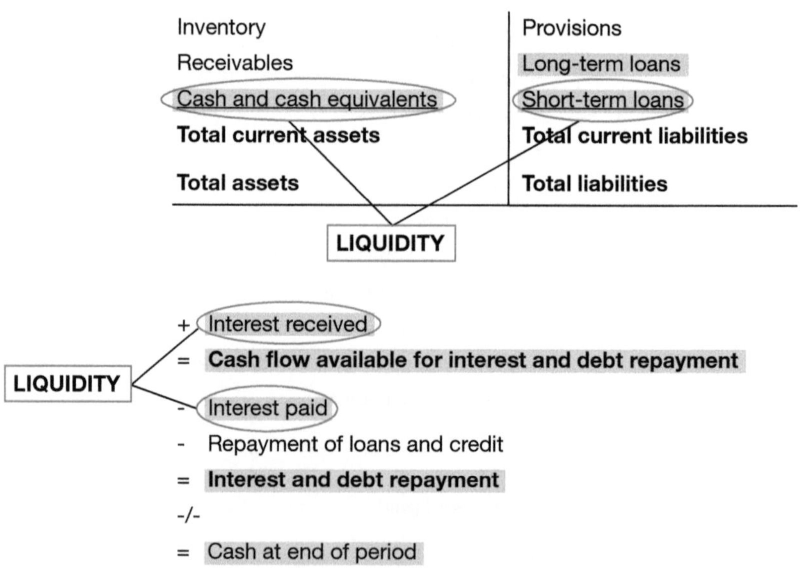

Whether a firm has sufficient liquidity can be determined in two ways:

- Dynamic liquidity
- Static liquidity

Dynamic liquidity

Dynamic liquidity shows whether the incoming cash flow is more or less than the outgoing cash flow over a particular period in the future. You need to have inside information on a firm to be able to determine the dynamic liquidity. On the basis of estimates of the major cash flows within the firm, a projection can be made of the development of the cash flows that will be available to the firm for several years in advance.

The sum of the cash flows and the unused portion of committed debt facilities shows the total liquidity that can be used immediately.

Static liquidity

Static liquidity shows whether a firm can meet its short-term obligations through use of its current assets. The static liquidity can be calculated using ratios that can be derived from the balance sheet. Since the data in the balance sheet are a snapshot in time, these figures are known as static.

I prefer dynamic liquidity over static liquidity because the former is based on real cash flows and not on accounting items.

Static liquidity can be measured by liquidity ratios. They are calculated on the basis of balance sheet items that can be rapidly turned into cash. The items in question are current assets and current liabilities:

Current assets

Current assets comprise three items:

- Inventory
- Debtors
- Cash and cash equivalents

Of all current assets, cash and cash equivalents (money placed in the money market) are the most liquid: they can usually be used immediately by the firm to pay invoices or salaries. Debtors are less liquid. Debtors represent goods or services provided by the firm for which the invoice still has to be paid. There is however no certainty that the debtors will actually pay, or when exactly they will pay. Only once the payment is received does a debtor move to cash in the balance sheet. Inventory is the least liquid of these items.

Inventory is held for future sale to customers. The question is: when will the inventory be sold and at what price? On sale, inventory becomes a debtor, which in turn eventually becomes cash. In other words, there is a degree of uncertainty attached to the conversion of inventory and debtors into cash. The uncertainty especially applies to outsiders, as they have no insight into the events behind the items in the balance sheet.

Current liabilities

Current liabilities consist of two items:

- Creditors
- Other current liabilities

Current liabilities concern obligations to third parties that the firm has to pay within one year. Creditors are those who have supplied goods or services to the firm that still have to be paid for. Other current liabilities relate, for instance, to repayments of short-term bank credit, long-term loans falling due within one year and tax that is due.

The cash for the payment of current liabilities has to be generated from the current assets. A firm's liquidity is therefore a combination of its current assets and its current liabilities. A firm can increase its cash balance by the following means:

- Take longer to pay suppliers (increases creditors)
- Collect from debtors more quickly (decreases debtors)
- Process inventory more quickly (decreases inventory)

Various measures are used to determine a firm's liquidity. The advantage of using liquidity ratios is that you can analyse the results over time and compare the results with those of other companies. There are three commonly used liquidity measures:

1. Current ratio
2. Quick ratio
3. Net working capital

1. Current ratio

The current ratio is calculated as follows:

Current ratio = current assets / current liabilities

The ratio between the current assets and the current liabilities must be at least 1 if the firm wishes to be able to fully pay its current liabilities out of its current assets. The point to be remembered is: creditors, long-term loans that have to be repaid within one year and short-term liabilities are actual payment obligations that a firm cannot avoid. These payments will be made by converting inventory and debtors into cash. The risk is that the inventory is worth less than its balance sheet value, or that creditors will not pay, or not pay in full. In other words, you have to know what is behind the numbers in order to be able to form a good opinion as to whether conversion of the book value of the inventory and the debtors into cash is a realistic proposition. If you don't have this information you could apply a buffer to the current ratio and look for a higher number, such as 1.3.

Table 5.1

Current ratio: Trader

Year-end 2013	€105,360,000 / €60,117,000 = 1.75
Year-end 2012	€91,260,000 / €41,904,000 = 2.18
Year-end 2011	€87,225,000 / €55,188,000 = 1.58

Assuming that Trader will realistically be able to convert its inventory and debtors into cash in the short term, it can be concluded that Trader had sufficient liquidity in all years on the basis of its current ratio.

As I mentioned above, using the current ratio can have disadvantages with regard to inventory. First, the assumption that inventory can be converted into cash in the short term. Second, the question whether the liquidation of inventory will achieve the book value in the balance sheet (in the event of a forced sale). To remove the effect of inventory, you can alternatively use the quick ratio.

2. Quick ratio

The quick ratio, also known as the acid test ratio, is the ratio between (i) current assets less inventory and (ii) current liabilities. The minimum required level is usually 1: the cash and receivables should be sufficient to pay the current liabilities in full.

The quick ratio is calculated as follows:

Quick ratio = (current assets – inventory) / current liabilities

Table 5.2 **Quick ratio: Trader**

Year-end 2013	(€105,360,000 – €60,696,000) / €60,117,000 = 0.74
Year-end 2012	(€91,260,000 – €53,406,000) / €41,904,000 = 0.90
Year-end 2011	(€87,225,000 – €49,143,000) / €55,188,000 = 0.69

Based on the standard of 1 for the quick ratio, Trader's liquidity position is insufficient. The poorer liquidity position based on the quick ratio in comparison to the current ratio is due to the relatively high level of inventory in comparison to the total current assets.

Note the payment term for debtors and creditors. If the payment term for debtors is longer than that for creditors, a (temporary) liquidity problem can still occur even if the result of the quick ratio is 1.

The disadvantage of ratios in general and liquidity ratios in particular is that they are easy to manipulate. Assume that Trader considered its quick ratio of 0.74 at year-end 2013 too low. It could have improved the ratio by waiting to pay its outstanding accounts until after 31 December. Assume that in the last quarter of 2013 a sum of €7,500,000 is paid out of cash to repay short-term debt. If Trader had not done this, €9,435,000 (€1,935,000 + €7,500,000) would have remained in cash and the short-term debt at balance sheet date would have stood at €67,617,000 (€60,117,000 + €7,500,000).

Table 5.3 **Quick ratio after manipulation: Trader**

Year-end 2013 new situation:	(€105,360,000 – €60,696,000 + €7,500,000) / €67,617,000 = 0.77
Year-end 2013 old situation:	(€105,360,000 – €60,696,000) / €60,117,000 = 0.74

Delaying the payment has slightly improved the quick ratio. Manipulation of liquidity calculations can be prevented by using absolute numbers, such as the net working capital, rather than ratios.

3. Net working capital

To calculate the net working capital, the current liabilities are subtracted from the current assets rather than divided by the current assets. This gives an absolute number rather than a ratio.

The formula for calculating the net working capital is:

Net working capital = current assets – current liabilities

Table 5.4

Net working capital: Trader

Year-end 2013	€105,360,000 – €60,117,000 = €45,243,000
Year-end 2012	€91,260,000 – €41,904,000 = €49,356,000
Year-end 2011	€87,225,000 – €55,188,000 = €32,037,000

A positive net working capital means that the current liabilities can be paid. Trader's net working capital was positive in the period from 2011 to 2013. However one still has to take a critical view of the quality of the inventory and debtors.

As you can see in Table 5.5, postponing payments in the fourth quarter to the next year has no effect on the calculation of the net working capital.

Table 5.5

Net working capital: Trader

Year-end 2013 new situation	(€105,360,000 + €7,500,000) – (€60,117,000 + €7,500,000) = €15,081,000
Year-end 2013 old situation	€105,360,000 – €60,117,000 = €15,081,000

To get a broader picture of the balance sheet and the liquidity position, you can also calculate the net working capital in a different way.

Alternative calculation of net working capital:

Net working capital = (equity + provisions + long-term loan capital) – non-current assets

If net working capital is a positive value on the basis of this formula, more equity and long-term loan capital has been raised than invested in non-current assets.

SOLVENCY

Solvency is indirectly influenced by interest rate risk as interest is ultimately, via net profit, incorporated in equity. In contrast to liquidity that focuses on short-term obligations, solvency is an important measure to assess whether a firm is able to survive in the long term: as a result solvency is often used as a financial covenant in financing agreements.

Solvency is an indication of the degree to which a firm can meet its obligations to the providers of loan capital in the event of liquidation. Many financing agreements contain a solvency ratio as a financial covenant, thus emphasising the importance of sufficient solvency for the financial health of a business. Solvency is often linked to a firm's ability to borrow: the higher its solvency, the more potential a firm has to raise new loan capital.

Figure 5.5 **Solvency**

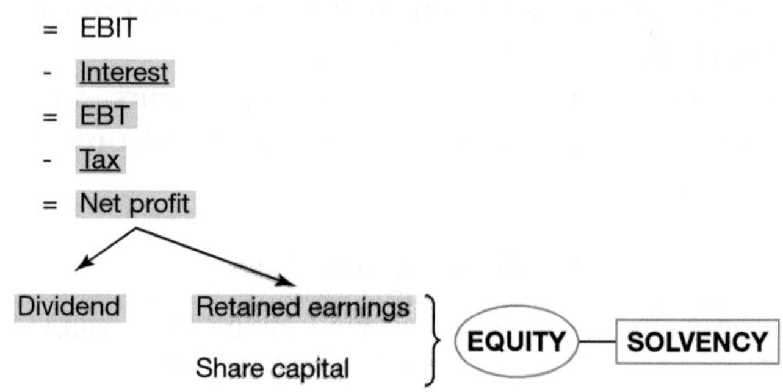

Solvency ratios

Solvency can be calculated in various ways. The most common ratio used in financing arrangements is the solvency ratio. We'll examine this ratio and two other solvency ratios:

1. Solvency ratio
2. Debt ratio
3. Gearing

1. Solvency ratio

The solvency ratio is the ratio between two capital components, namely equity and total balance sheet:

Solvency ratio = equity / balance sheet total

This ratio indicates whether the providers of loan capital can be repaid in the event of liquidation. A solvency ratio of at least 25% is usually required. Of course this depends on the individual firm and the business in which it operates.

Solvency ratio: Trader

Table 5.6

Year-end 2013	€36,666,000 / €136,416,000 = 26.9%
Year-end 2012	€35,313,000 / €118,188,000 = 29.9%
Year-end 2011	€33,876,000 / €104,364,000 = 32.5%

Trader meets the objective of a minimum solvency ratio of 25%. Trader's solvency clearly declined between 2011 and 2013 as a result of a greater increase in the total balance sheet of 30.7% ((€136,416,000 – €104,364,000) / €104,364,000) than equity increase, which was 8.3% in the same period ((€36,666,000 – €33,867,000) / €33,867,000).

2. Debt ratio

The debt ratio is related to the solvency ratio. The theory behind the debt ratio is that the higher the debt, the more difficult it is to meet debt service obligations. Note that provisions are considered as loan capital. The formula for calculating the debt ratio is:

> Debt ratio = (provisions + long-term loan capital + short-term loan capital) / total balance sheet

Debt ratio: Trader

Table 5.7

Year-end 2013	(€4,014,000 + €35,409,000 + €60,117,000) / €136,416,000 = 73%
Year-end 2012	(€2,856,000 + €37,956,000 + €41,904,000) / €118,188,000 = 70%
Year-end 2011	(€2,418,000 + €12,810,000 + €55,188,000) / €104,364,000 = 67.5%

Since the debt ratio and the solvency ratio are extensions of each other, the result for the debt ratio is in line with that for the solvency ratio: between 2011 and 2013 the debt increased more relative to the increase of the total balance sheet.

3. Gearing

The ratio between loan capital and equity is also used as an alternative to the solvency ratio (equity in relation to total balance sheet) and the debt ratio (loan capital in relation to total balance sheet). This ratio is known as gearing or leverage. The formula for calculating gearing is:

Gearing = loan capital / equity

Table 5.8 **Gearing: Trader**

Year-end 2013	(€4,014,000 + €35,409,000 + €60,117,000) / €36,666,000 = 271.5%
Year-end 2012	(€2,856,000 + €37,956,000 + €41,904,000) / €35,313,000 = 234.2%
Year-end 2011	(€2,418,000 + €12,810,000 + €55,188,000) / €33,867,000 = 207.9%

These results are of course in line with those for the solvency ratio and the debt ratio: between 2011 and 2013 loan capital increased faster than equity.

FINANCIAL COVENANTS

Financial covenants, such as the Interest Coverage Ratio (ICR), the net debt / EBITDA and the Debt Service Coverage Ratio (DSCR), are directly influenced by interest rate risk while the solvency ratio is indirectly influenced. Financial covenants are often part of a financing arrangement and a breach of a financial covenant allows the lender to call in its loans. As a result firms are very aware of financial covenants. Hedging interest rate risk is a way of mitigating the risk of breaching a financial covenant.

A financial covenant is actually a ratio. The term 'financial covenant' is used as soon as the ratio is included in a financing arrangement as a covenant. Once this happens, the ratio is not simply an indication of the financial status of a firm – there are also consequences involved if the covenant is broken. In principle, the bank is entitled to call in the facility immediately in such a situation. For this reason, financial covenants are the subject of much attention during the negotiation process and during the life of loans.

Because financial covenants are often based on accounting numbers, you are able to exactly calculate the situation when a financial covenant will be breached. This implies that you know upfront what movements in interest rates lead to a breach.

Financial covenants

Figure 5.6

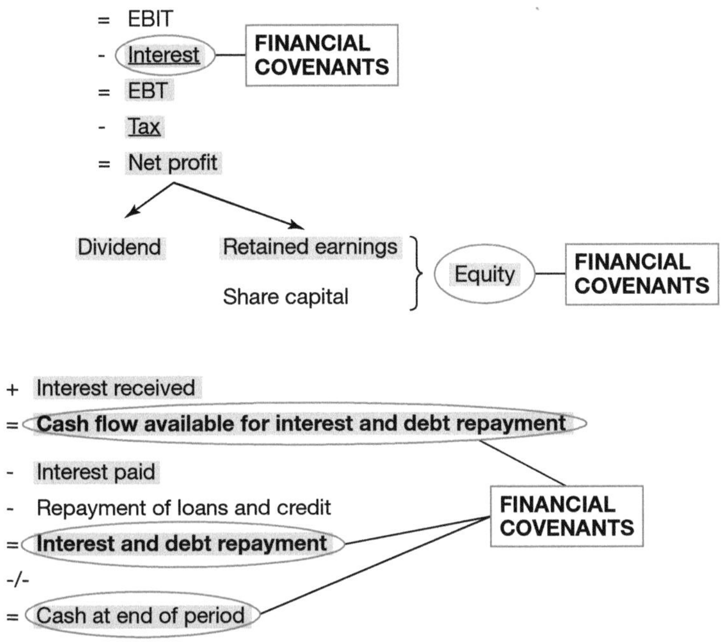

Commonly used financial covenants

In financing agreements the solvency ratio, the ICR and the net debt / EBITDA ratio are often used as financial covenants. In the case of M&A transactions and project finance the DSCR is commonly used. Therefore, we'll examine these four frequently used ratios:

1. Solvency ratio
2. ICR
3. Net debt / EBITDA
4. DSCR

1. Solvency ratio

The solvency ratio has already been discussed. Therefore, I will only give a brief summary here. Solvency is defined as the ratio between a firm's equity and its balance sheet total. The solvency ratio shows the extent to which a firm is able to meet its obligations to the providers of loan capital. The higher the ratio, the better the firm is able to repay the borrowed funds out of its assets.

Interest has an effect on equity: the lower the interest payable, the higher the net profit and retained earnings (equity). Of course, a firm may also choose to distribute the higher net profit to its shareholders in the form of dividend.

2. ICR

The ICR shows the operating result (EBIT) as a multiple of the interest payable. The ratio is calculated by dividing the operating result by the interest payable (both items in the income statement). The higher the ratio the better, since it is then less likely that the firm will fail to meet its interest payment obligations and therefore encounter financial difficulties.

If a bank provides financing to a firm, its main concern is that interest and principal repayment obligations are met throughout the term of the loan. If a firm (temporarily) does not have sufficient means to meet its repayment obligations, in most cases a solution can be found. The situation is more serious if a firm cannot meet its interest obligations. This means that there is a serious imbalance between the firm's (operating) income and its interest-bearing debt. Failure to maintain the required ICR is therefore often a sign of (serious) financial problems. Trader needs to comply with a minimum ICR of 3. If the ICR is lower than 1, this obviously means there is an urgent problem since the firm's income is no longer sufficient to meet its interest obligations.

The formula for calculating the ICR is:

Interest Coverage Ratio (ICR) = EBIT / interest payable

Table 5.9 **ICR: Trader**

2014	€9,087,000 / €3,561,000 = 2.55
2013	€8,604,000 / €3,396,000 = 2.53
2012	€6,933,000 / €2,646,000 = 2.62

Trader's ICR is just sufficient to meet the required minimum of 3.

3. Net debt / EBITDA

The net debt / EBITDA ratio shows the ratio between a firm's net debt position and its earnings before interest, tax, depreciation and amortisation (EBITDA). Net debt is the sum of all interest-bearing liabilities, such as short- and long-term loans, minus the cash. Cash is directly influenced by interest payments and receipts. The theory behind this ratio is that the debt has to be repaid out of the operating profit. EBITDA is a proxy of this. The lower the ratio, the better the firm is able to meet its repayment obligations. Normally the required level for the net debt / EBITDA ratio is a maximum of 3.

The net debt / EBITDA ratio is a comparison between an item from the balance sheet and an item from the income statement. The formula is as follows:

Net debt / EBITDA = (interest-bearing liabilities – cash) / EBITDA

Table 5.10

Net debt / EBITDA ratio: Trader

2013	(€35,409,000 + €2,631,000 + €22,668,000 – €1,935,000) / €10,935,000 = 5.4
2012	(€37,956,000 + €2,667,000 + €9,885,000 – €2,673,000) / €8,829,000 = 5.4
2011	(€12,810,000 + €2,235,000 + €30,306,000 – €2,226,000) / €11,631,000 = 3.7

The net debt / EBITDA ratio deteriorated between 2011 and 2012 as a result of a combination of rising net debt and, more importantly, a decline in EBITDA. Between 2012 and 2013 the ratio was stable. However both net debt and EBITDA increased sharply.

4. DSCR

The Debt Service Coverage Ratio (DSCR) is the ratio between the cash flow available for interest and debt repayment and the debt service. The DSCR is therefore a financial covenant that is completely based on cash flow. The formula is:

Debt Service Coverage Ratio (DSCR) = cash flow available for interest and debt repayment / debt service

The result must be at least 1. If it is less than 1, the firm is not able to meet its interest and debt repayment obligations. This ratio is usually applied to project and acquisition finance. This is because it usually involves substantial financing in comparison to equity and the loans provided are normally determined exactly on the basis of the firm's projected future cash flows.

Corporate finance teams involved in mergers and acquisitions make models of the firm's expected cash flows after an acquisition.

The debt burden that the firm can bear is then calculated on the basis of its expected cash flows.

An example of a DSCR analysis is given below. The items in bold type, 'Cash flow available for interest and debt repayment' and 'Interest and debt repayment', form the components of the DSCR.

Cash at beginning of period
+ Sales
- Purchases
- Salaries
- Other expenses
- Investments
- Acquisitions
+ Disposals
+/- Issue/repurchase of own shares
+ New loans and drawdowns of credit
- Repayments of loans/credits
+ Repayments of loans/credits granted
- Provision of loans/credits granted
+ Grants
- Tax
- Dividend paid
+ Interest received
= **Cash flow available for interest and debt repayment**

- Interest paid
- Repayment of loans and credit
= **Interest and debt repayment**
-/-
= Cash at end of period

CASH CYCLE

A firm's cash cycle is influenced by interest rate risk through two channels:

- Interest payable and receivable influences the cash position.

- The cash and cash equivalents item in the balance sheet is likely to be exposed to interest rate risk.

The cash cycle, or cash conversion cycle, comprises all the phases a firm goes through to convert the cash invested in the firm in the form of procurement, production and sales into a larger sum of money. The cash cycle starts at the time the procurement invoices are paid and ends when the receivables from customers are collected. For the firm it is important to keep the cash cycle as short as possible. A short cash cycle implies that the firm's free cash flow is always quickly available.

Figure 5.7

Cash cycle

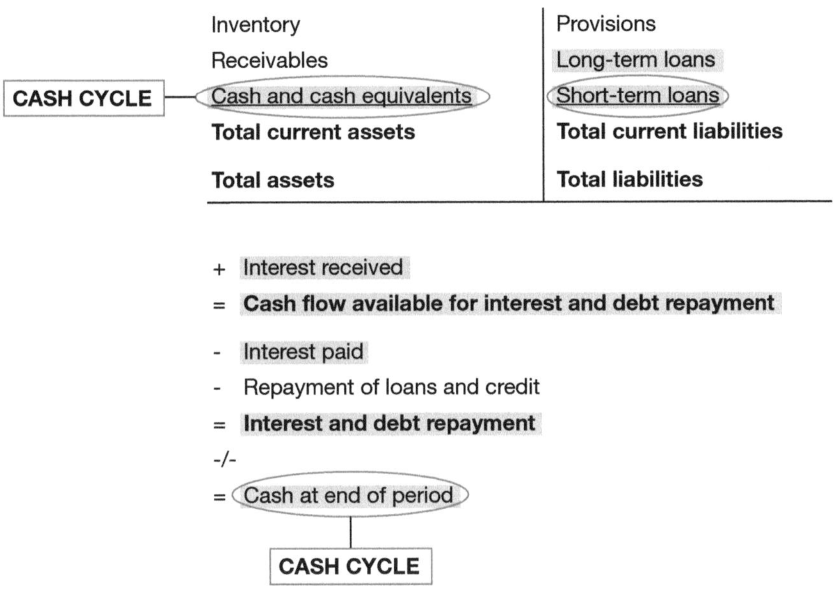

A firm can influence the amount of cash locked up in the cash cycle by actively managing its working capital. Using ratios, you can obtain an impression of how a firm's cash cycle operates.

Five cash cycle ratios are:

1. Average term of credit received
2. Average term of credit allowed
3. Inventory turnover time
4. The cash cycle
5. Turnover ratios

1. Average term of credit received

The average term of credit received shows the time taken by a firm to pay its suppliers. It is calculated as follows:

Term of credit received (in days) = creditors / purchases on account × 365

The longer the term of credit received, the lower the cash requirement and the more it is to the firm's advantage. This is because the firm receives interest on cash as long as it is in its own account and the firm has a cash surplus. If the firm borrows money, it can draw the credit at a later date if the term of credit received is longer. The income statement for 2014 is available; however, because no balance sheet data for 2014 are available, the term of credit received for the period 2011–13 is used for calculations.

Table 5.11 **Average term of credit received: Trader**

2013	€25,158,000 / €204,894,000 × 365 = 45 days
2012	€20,646,000 / €178,881,000 × 365 = 42 days
2011	€13,281,000 / €164,994,000 × 365 = 29 days

The term of credit received by Trader increased between 2011 and 2013. This is good for Trader because a higher creditors' total reduces the drain on the firm's cash.

A firm can take the following three steps to increase its term of credit received:

- Negotiate better terms of delivery
- Make more use of supplier credit
- Pay on the last due date

2. Average term of credit allowed

The average term of credit allowed is the average time that passes between the existence of receivables and their collection. The formula is:

Term of credit allowed (in days) = debtors / sales on account × 365

The debtors are a drain on the firm's cash. Shortening the term of credit allowed leads to a lower debtors' total and therefore less of a drain on cash.

Average term of credit allowed: Trader

Table 5.12

2013	€39,579,000 / €266,613,000 × 365 = 54 days
2012	€32,646,000 / €235,752,000 × 365 = 51 days
2011	€32,607,000 / €221,352,000 × 365 = 54 days

The term of credit allowed by Trader remained more or less constant between 2011 and 2013. What is notable is that between 2011 and 2013 the average term of credit received was lower than the average term of credit allowed. This is negative for Trader's cash position.

A firm can take five steps to reduce its term of credit allowed:

- Shorten its credit period
- Offer a discount for quick payment
- Accelerate the invoice process
- Improve its debtor administration
- Tighten up its collection policy

3. Inventory turnover time

The inventory turnover time shows how long the firm's total inventory exists on average. It is calculated as follows:

Inventory turnover time (in days) = inventory / cost of sales × 365

Inventory with a longer turnover time remains on the balance sheet longer and places a bigger drain on cash than inventory that turns over quickly. For this reason, it is to a firm's advantage to retain as low a level of inventory as possible.

Inventory turnover time: Trader

Table 5.13

2013	€60,696,000 / €204,894,000 × 365 = 108 days
2012	€53,406,000 / €178,881,000 × 365 = 109 days
2011	€49,143,000 / €164,994,000 × 365 = 109 days

Trader's inventory turnover time remained more or less constant between 2011 and 2013.

A firm can take two steps to reduce its inventory turnover time:

- Improve its inventory administration
- Order its inventory on a just-in-time basis

4. The cash cycle

The cash cycle is the result of the average terms of debtors, inventory and creditors. If you know these terms, you can calculate the total length of the cash cycle:

	average term of credit allowed
+	inventory turnover time
-/-	average term of credit received
=	length of the cash cycle

Based on the values of these variables calculated for Trader, the length of the cash cycle is as follows:

Table 5.14

Cash cycle: Trader

2013	54 days + 108 days – 45 days = 117 days
2012	51 days + 109 days – 42 days = 118 days
2011	54 days + 109 days – 29 days = 134 days

Trader's cash cycle accelerated between 2011 and 2012, mainly due to an increase in the term of credit received.

A firm can save interest by shortening its cash cycle. The next example demonstrates how much Trader could save by shortening the term of credit allowed, assuming an interest rate of 3%.

The firm's net working capital in 2013 is (€105,360,000 – €60,117,000) = €45,243,000. The annual interest due on this amount of working capital is: €45,243,000 × 3% = €1,357,290. Now you will see how much interest Trader could save if it succeeds in getting its debtors to pay more quickly by increasing efficiency.

The average term of credit allowed is 54 days in 2013. Let's assume that Trader manages to reduce this by 14 days. The average term of credit allowed then becomes 40 days. This means that the debtors' total is lower. First, calculate how much the reduction will be as a result of shortening the collection time. For this, the formula for average term of credit allowed is:

Term of credit allowed (in days) = debtors / sales on account × 365
becomes:
Debtors = (term of credit allowed x sales on account) / 365

The new value for the debtors item is: (40 x €266,613,000) / 365 = €29,217,863. This implies a reduction of €10,361,137 (€39,579,000 – €29,217,863); the drain on the firm's cash is reduced by an equal amount. The reduction in the interest the firm has to pay each year is: €10,361,137 × 3% = €310,834.

So, by reducing its collection of receivables by two weeks, Trader can save €310,834 in interest payments. This shows the importance of efficient working capital management. Obviously, the amount of interest saved depends on the interest rate. A similar calculation can be made for the potential saving from a reduction in the inventory turnover time or an extension of the average term of credit received.

5. Turnover ratios

As discussed, the average term of credit received, the inventory turnover time and the average term of credit allowed show how long cash is tied up in various balance sheet items. A ratio related to these measures is the turnover ratio. I'll be discussing three turnover ratios:

- Inventory turnover ratio
- Receivables turnover ratio
- Payables turnover ratio

Inventory turnover ratio

The inventory turnover ratio shows how quickly the assets invested in inventory become available. The sales are divided by the average inventory:

Inventory turnover ratio = cost of sales / inventory

Table 5.15

Inventory turnover ratio: Trader

2013	€204,894,000 / €60,696,000 = 3.38
2012	€178,881,000 / €53,406,000 = 3.35
2011	€164,994,000 / €49,143,000 = 3.36

In 2013 Trader's inventory was sold 3.38 times per year. The higher the turnover ratio and therefore the shorter the turnover time, the less working capital is required and therefore the better the liquidity position. The inventory turnover ratio can also be calculated by dividing 365 days by the inventory turnover time (in this case 108 days).

Receivables turnover ratio

The receivables turnover ratio shows how quickly the debtors make their payments. The higher the ratio, the faster the debtors pay and thus the better the firm's liquidity position becomes. To calculate the receivables turnover ratio, sales are divided by the average accounts receivable:

Receivables turnover ratio = sales on account / accounts receivable

Table 5.16 **Receivables turnover ratio: Trader**

2013	€266,613,000 / €39,579,000 = 6.74
2012	€235,752,000 / €32,646,000 = 7.22
2011	€221,352,000 / €32,607,000 = 6.79

In 2013 Trader received cash inflow amounting to 6.74 times its average accounts receivable. The receivables turnover ratio can also be calculated by dividing 365 days by the average term of credit allowed (54 days). Note: the average term of credit allowed is rounded off. Efficient receivables management leads to a higher turnover ratio.

Payables turnover ratio

The payables turnover ratio shows how quickly the firm pays its creditors. The lower the payables turnover ratio, the longer the period in which the firm can use supplier credit and the better the firm's liquidity position will be.

The ratio is calculated as follows:

Payables turnover ratio = purchases on account / accounts payable

Table 5.17

Payables turnover ratio: Trader

2013	€204,894,000 / €25,158,000 = 8.14
2012	€178,881,000 / €20,646,000 = 8.66
2011	€164,994,000 / €13,281,000 = 12.42

Trader paid its accounts payable balance 8.14 times in 2013. The payables turnover ratio can also be calculated by dividing 365 days by the average term of credit received.

PROFITABILITY

A firm's profitability is influenced by interest rate risk because in the income statement interest payable and receivable trickles through to net profit. Profitability is the relationship between a firm's capital and its net profit. Profitability is often related to Return On Equity, but there are other meaningful profitability ratios that we'll discuss. In the end a firm wants to ensure that both equity and loan capital providers are happy in the long run.

Figure 5.8

Profitability

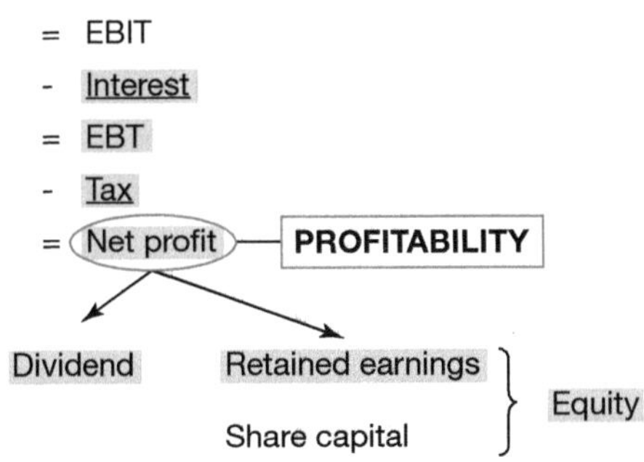

For a firm to have continuity, it must generate sufficient earnings over the long term to be able to pay dividend and/or interest to its capital providers (shareholders and loan providers).

We'll examine the following profitability ratios:

1. Return on assets
2. Weighted average cost of loan capital
3. Return on equity
4. Profit margin

1. Return on assets

A firm's assets consist of loan capital and equity. After deducting all expenses from turnover, apart from interest, there must be a surplus to pay the providers of these two types of assets.

Return on assets (ROA) is calculated by dividing the balance of the pre-tax profit and interest by the assets invested in the year in question:

> Return on assets (ROA) = (pre-tax profit + interest) / average total assets × 100%

Total assets is the same as the total balance sheet. You can only calculate Trader's return on assets for 2012 and 2013 as you do not have the balance sheet data for 2010 (needed to calculate the average total assets in 2011).

Table 5.18

Return on assets: Trader

2013	(€5,280,000 + €3,396,000) / ((€136,416,000 + €118,188,000) / 2) = 6.82%
2012	€4,383,000 + €2,646,000) / ((€118,188,000 + €104,364,000) / 2) = 6.32%

The ROA shows that for each unit invested in the firm, a surplus of almost 7% remains in 2013. Part of this will be paid as interest to the providers of the loan capital. The rest, after deduction of corporation tax, will be paid to the providers of equity capital. The standard for a profit-oriented firm is simple: the higher the profitability, the better.

2. Weighted average cost of loan capital

The weighted average cost of loan capital (WACLC) concerns the interest paid on the (average) interest-bearing liabilities. This number shows the average cost of the loan capital the firm has raised, and is calculated as follows:

> Weighted average cost of loan capital (WACLC) = interest paid / average loan capital invested

The average loan capital invested is the difference between the average total capital invested and the average equity invested.

Weighted average cost of loan capital: Trader

Table 5.19

2013	€3,396,000 / ((€99,750,000 + €82,875,000) / 2) = 3.72%
2012	€2,646,000 / ((€82,875,000 + €70,497,000) / 2) = 3.45%

Trader's providers of loan capital received interest at an average rate of 3.72% in 2013.

3. Return on equity

Return on equity (ROE) is determined by relating earnings to the average equity capital invested. Usually the figure for earnings before deduction of corporation tax is used:

Return on equity (ROE) = pre-tax profit / average equity capital

For the pre-tax profit, use EBT (Earnings Before Taxes) from the income statement. Equity is taken from the balance sheet (shown as total net worth).

Return on equity: Trader

Table 5.20

2013	€5,280,000 / ((€36,666,000 + €35,313,000) / 2) = 14.67%
2012	€4,383,000 / ((€35,313,000 + €33,867,000) / 2) = 12.67%

Each unit of equity delivered a net profit (before tax) to shareholders of nearly 15% in 2013.

Financial leverage

There is a relationship between profitability and solvency, which is shown by the financial leverage ratio.

In Trader's case, the return on assets was 6.82% in 2013 and the return on equity was 14.67%. Equity, which is part of the total assets, therefore generated a higher return than the total assets. This is because on each unit of operating result, interest has first to be paid on the loan capital. The remainder goes to the shareholders. The lower the interest paid in relation to the return on assets and the higher the ratio of loan capital and equity, the greater the degree of financial leverage. The formula for this relationship is as follows (note there are rounding differences in the calculations):

ROE = ROA + (ROA – WACLC) loan capital / equity

Table 5.21 **ROE: Trader**

2013	14.67% = 6.82% + (6.82% – 3.72%) €91,312,500 / €35,989,500
2012	12.67% = 6.32% + (6.32% – 3.45%) €76,686,000 / €34,590,000

As the solvency (shown by loan capital/equity) deteriorates, the return on equity increases. The reverse is true if the average interest rate increases to a level higher than the return on assets.

4. Profit margin

The profit margin is the relationship between sales and profit – in other words, the percentage of sales remaining as profit for the firm. There are three types of profit margin:

- Gross profit margin
- Operating profit margin
- Net profit margin

The difference between the gross profit margin and the operating profit margin is that the gross profit margin shows the proportion of sales available to cover the indirect expenses. The operating profit on the other hand shows the proportion of sales remaining for the firm's financiers (providers of loan capital and equity). The net profit margin shows the proportion of sales remaining for the shareholders. Profit margins vary widely between the various industries. Trading firms are expected to generate lower profit margins, while capital-intensive firms are expected to have higher profit margins.

Gross profit margin

The gross profit margin shows the percentage of sales remaining after the firm has paid its costs of sales:

Gross profit margin = (sales – costs of sales) / sales × 100%

For sales, use the net sales as shown in the income statement, and for the costs of sales use the third party item. In fact the gross income is divided by the sales.

Table 5.22

Gross profit margin: Trader

2014	(€281,571,000 – €213,003,000) / €281,571,000 = 24.35%
2013	(€266,613,000 – €204,894,000) / €266,613,000 = 23.15%
2012	(€235,752,000 – €178,881,000) / €235,752,000 = 24.12%
2011	(€221,352,000 – €164,994,000) / €221,352,000 = 25.46%

Trader's gross profit margin fell slightly between 2011 and 2014.

Operating profit margin

The operating profit margin shows the percentage of sales remaining after all expenses other than tax and interest expenses are deducted:

Operating profit margin = operating result (EBIT) / sales × 100%

For the operating result, use EBIT from the income statement and for sales use net sales.

Table 5.23

Operating profit margin: Trader

2014	€9,087,000 / €281,571,000 = 3.23%
2013	€8,604,000 / €266,613,000 = 3.23%
2012	€6,933,000 / €235,752,000 = 2.94%
2011	€9,774,000 / €221,352,000 = 4.42%

The operating profit margin fell between 2011 and 2012 and recovered in 2013 and 2014.

Net profit margin

The net profit margin shows the percentage of sales remaining after all expenses, including tax and interest, are deducted: this percentage actually shows the proportion of sales remaining for the shareholders. The net profit margin is calculated as follows:

Net profit margin = net profit / sales × 100%

For the net profit, take the income from the income statement and for sales take net sales.

Table 5.24 **Net profit margin: Trader**

2014	€3,546,000 / €281,571,000 = 1.26%
2013	€3,312,000 / €266,613,000 = 1.24%
2012	€2,763,000 / €235,752,000 = 1.17%
2011	€4,893,000 / €221,352,000 = 2.21%

Trader's net profit margin declined sharply after 2011.

SHARE PRICE RATIOS

One further area that is influenced by interest rate risk is share price ratios. Interest rate risk influences share price ratios because interest payable and receivable affects three important elements of share price ratios:

- Net profit.
- Dividend.
- Retained earnings. Lower interest payable leads to higher net profits. The firm can choose to pay out higher dividends or to increase the retained earnings.

Share price ratios are often used for listed firms, but also give valuable information for the non-listed firm because they can be used to compare a firm with its peers.

Figure 5.9 **Share price ratios**

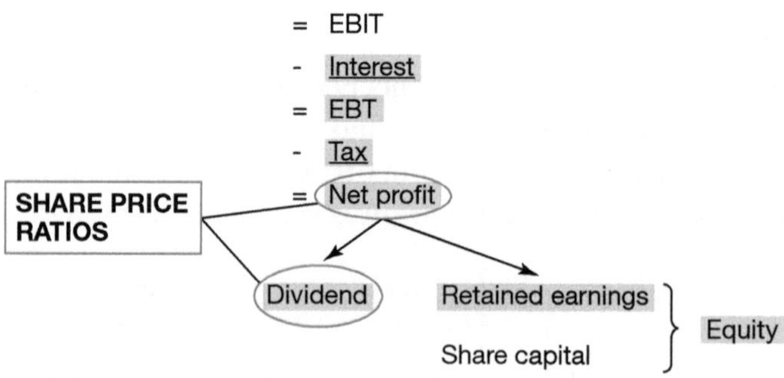

The following five share price ratios are discussed:

1. Earnings per share
2. Price/earnings ratio

3. Dividend yield
4. Total shareholder return
5. Pay-out ratio per share

1. Earnings per share

Earnings per share (EPS) shows the net earnings available for dividend distribution per share:

Earnings per share (EPS) = net income / number of issued shares

EPS: Trader

Trader generated net earnings of €3,312,000 in 2013. Trader issued three million shares. This gives an EPS (rounded off) of €1.10 (€3,312,000 / 3,000,000).

2. Price/earnings ratio

The price/earnings ratio (P/E) is often used to measure a firm's valuation. The price/earnings ratio is determined by dividing the share price by the earnings per share. The price/earnings ratio shows the multiple of a firm's earnings that investors are prepared to pay in the market.

Price/earnings ratio (P/E) = share price / earnings per share

The P/Es of firms may vary widely. A business expected to show strong earnings growth will have a higher price/earnings ratio than a business whose earnings are expected to remain more or less the same.

P/E: Trader

Based on a share price of €10, Trader's price/earnings ratio would be 9.09 (€10/€1.10). In other words, an investor purchasing the share for €10 is paying 9.09 times the EPS. Whether this is cheap or expensive depends on the P/Es of similar companies and of the market as a whole.

3. Dividend yield

Dividend yield is the return on shares on the basis of the dividend distributed. The dividend yield is calculated by dividing the total amount of dividend distributed during the year by the current share price:

Dividend yield = dividend per share / current share price × 100%

The dividend yield ratio is mostly useful in the assessment of shares that generate low capital gains, rather than shares whose performance is reflected in their price movement. While future dividend payments are uncertain, most companies strive to distribute a stable or slightly increasing level of dividend.

Dividend yield: Trader

Trader had net earnings of €3,312,000 in 2013 and distributed a total of €1,959,000 as dividend. The dividend per share therefore comes to €0.65 (€1,959,000 / 3,000,000 shares).

4. Total shareholder return

The yield realised on holding shares, known as the total shareholder return (TSR), is calculated as follows:

Total shareholder return (TSR) = (sale price – purchase price + dividend) / purchase price × 100%

TSR is thus the sum of the price movement and the dividend paid.

TSR: Trader

Trader's share price rose from €9 to €10 in 2013. As calculated earlier, Trader's dividend yield is €0.65. Trader's TSR is calculated as follows: (€10 – €9 + €0.65) / €9 = 18.3%.

5. Pay-out ratio per share

The pay-out ratio per share is a variation of the dividend yield ratio. The calculation of the dividend yield is significantly determined by the share price in the market. To eliminate this uncertain factor, one can use the pay-out ratio. The pay-out ratio shows the proportion of net earnings distributed as dividend:

$$\text{Pay-out ratio} = \text{dividend} / \text{net earnings} \times 100\%$$

Pay-out ratio: Trader

Out of its net earnings of €3,312,000 in 2013, Trader added a total of €1,353,000 to its reserves and distributed €1,959,000 as dividend. Its pay-out ratio was therefore 59.1% (€1,959,000 / €3,312,000).

Part 4

HEDGING MAKES SENSE UNDER SPECIFIC CIRCUMSTANCES ONLY

INTRODUCTION TO PART 4

The key learning outcome in Part 4 is that you will understand when hedging increases firm value – thus, when it will make sense and when it won't. Part 4 is the third out of four stages in a firm's interest rate risk management process.

Hedging does not make sense under all circumstances. If a firm hedges for the wrong reasons, hedging may even decrease instead of increase firm value because hedging costs money! As I have said, a necessary condition for a firm to create value with hedging is that it is exposed to interest rate risk. However, being exposed to interest rate risk alone is not sufficient. In this part I will explain to you the conditions under which hedging does create firm value and therefore makes sense.

The benefits of hedging are based on corporate finance theory. I'll first take you back in time. In their seminal work in 1958 Modigliani and Miller argue, focusing initially on corporate finance decisions, that in a perfect capital market the market value of a firm is unaffected by its capital structure decisions (capital structure decisions relate to the optimal ratio of debt to equity).[1] Modigliani and Miller reason that capital structure decisions are irrelevant since in a perfect market they can be replicated by investors. Later the irrelevance propositions are extended to all financing decisions, including hedging. Thus, for instance, a firm's decision to hedge its exposure to interest rate risk will not affect the value of the firm as shareholders can achieve the same risk reduction through hedging themselves.

Modigliani and Miller's arguments for hedging to be irrelevant are based on the following necessary conditions:

- There are no taxes.
- There are no costs of bankruptcy.
- There are no transaction costs.
- Investors and the firm have equal access to financial markets and deal at the same price.

In modern corporate finance theory the framework presented by Modigliani and Miller still serves as an important benchmark. In 1998 Miller, 30 years later, observes: 'Looking back now, perhaps we should have put more emphasis on the other, upbeat side of the "nothing matters" coin: showing what *doesn't* matter can also show, by implication, what *does*.'[2] Therefore, if the conditions assumed by Modigliani and Miller are relaxed in the light of market imperfections, a firm can benefit from managing interest rate risk. Corporate finance theory identifies four areas where firms can benefit from hedging:

1. Reducing expected taxes
2. Minimising financial distress costs
3. Reducing agency costs
4. Controlling managerialism

We'll look at the rationale for hedging in each of the four areas separately, given the following assumptions:

- Firms hedge to decrease risk and not to speculate.
- Hedging is costless. In practice, hedging naturally is not costless and these costs should be incorporated: transaction costs, management costs and liquidity requirements from derivatives.
- Firms do not need to fully hedge interest rate risk in order to benefit from hedging. Partial hedging also increases firm value.

6

Hedging theory

REDUCING EXPECTED TAXES

The first reason for hedging interest rate risk is to reduce expected taxes. Hedging can reduce the expected taxes if the tax schedule is a convex rather than a linear function of income. A tax schedule is convex when the firm's average effective tax rate increases as pre-tax income increases, in other words if there is a progressive tax schedule.

Table 6.1 gives you a view of various countries around the world with a progressive corporate tax rate in 2014.[3]

Countries with a progressive corporate tax rate **Table 6.1**

Country	Progressive tax rate
Belgium	A lower progressive tax rate applies to companies that are more than 50% owned by individuals.
Brazil	The corporate income tax rate of 25% is a combination of a 15% basic rate and a 10% surtax on income that exceeds BRL240,000 per year.
Canada	The corporate income tax rate is 26.5%, comprising a 15% federal tax component and an 11.5% provincial tax component. Depending on the province, the combined general corporate income tax rate ranges from 25% to 31%. Lower corporate income tax rates are available to Canadian-controlled private corporations on their first CAD$500,000 of taxable active business income.
France	A 3.3% social contribution is levied on the part of the corporate income tax that exceeds €763,000, resulting in an overall maximum tax rate of 34.43%. In addition, a temporary 10.7% surtax is levied on the (full) corporate income tax for entities with a sales turnover greater than €250 million.
Hungary	A 10% corporate income tax rate applies for taxable income up to HUF 500 million. The excess is taxed at 19%.
Indonesia	Listed companies which meet certain conditions are eligible for a 5% reduction in the corporate tax rate. A company with gross turnover less than IDR 50 billion is eligible for a 50% reduction of the corporate tax rate on the proportion of taxable income which results when IDR 4.8 billion is divided by the gross annual turnover. Where gross turnover is below IDR 4.8 billion, the reduction applies on all taxable income.
Malaysia	Resident companies with a paid up capital of MYR 2.5 million and below are subject to a corporate income tax rate of 20% on the first MYR 500,000 of chargeable income. For chargeable income in excess of MYR 500,000, the corporate income tax rate is 25%.

Country	Progressive tax rate
Morocco	The corporate tax rate is 30%. Companies with a profit not exceeding 300,000 MAD benefit from a reduced corporate tax rate of 10%.
Netherlands	The corporate tax rate is 25%. The first €200,000 of taxable profit is taxed at 20%.
Spain	The corporate tax rate is 30%. Where a company's turnover in the immediately preceding tax period is less than €10 million, it is taxed on the first €300,000 of taxable income at 25% and the excess is taxed at 30%. Where a company's turnover in 2014 is less than €5 million and the average labour force from the 2009 to 2014 tax year is less than 25 employees, it is taxed on the first €300,000 of taxable income at 20% and the remaining at 25%.
United Kingdom	The corporate tax rate is 21%. A small companies rate of 20% applies until 1 April 2015 to companies with taxable profits of up to £300,000 with marginal relief up to £1.5 million. Companies with taxable profits of £1.5 million or more pay tax at the main rate.
United States	The corporate income tax rate is approximately 40%. The marginal federal corporate income tax rate on the highest income bracket of corporations (currently above US$18,333,333) is 35%.

The line of reasoning is that hedging reduces the volatility of pre-tax income. And, as taxes are higher in a situation of higher pre-tax profits than in a situation of lower pre-tax profits, this implies a lower average tax burden and a higher expected value of the firm after tax.

Convexity of the tax schedule can also be created by tax preference items, such as tax-loss carry-backs and carry-forwards. In the latter case, the relevant cost is the reduction in the present value of the tax benefits.

Example

Reducing expected taxes

A firm has a 20% rate on pre-tax profits between €0 and €500,000 and a rate of 25% on pre-tax profits above €500,000. The firm must pay corporation tax on two successive fiscal years. The tax burden is calculated with and without hedging interest rate risk. Pre-tax profits are the same in both cases, namely a total of €1,000,000 for the two-year period.

If the firm does not hedge, it has greater volatility in its pre-tax profits: €200,000 in year one and €800,000 in year two. The total tax burden over the two years then is (€200,000 × 20% in year one) + (€500,000 × 20% + €300,000 × 25% in year two) = €215,000. ▶

If the firm does hedge, pre-tax profit is the same in both years: €500,000. The total tax burden over the two years in that case is (€500,000 × 20% in year one) + (€500,000 × 20% in year two) = €200,000.

	Tax payable without hedging			Tax payable with hedging		
	Year 1	Year 2	Total	Year 1	Year 2	Total
Pre-tax profit	€200,000	€800,000	€1,000,000	€500,000	€500,000	€1,000,000
Tax	€40,000	€175,000	€215,000	€100,000	€100,000	€200,000
Net profit	€160,000	€625,000	€785,000	€400,000	€400,000	€800,000

Through hedging interest rate risk the firm saves €15,000 in corporation tax.

MINIMISING FINANCIAL DISTRESS COSTS

The second reason for hedging is to minimise financial distress costs. There are three types of direct and indirect costs associated with financial distress:

Financial distress costs

Financial distress is a situation in which a firm has insufficient cash to pay its financial obligations to third parties such as payments for goods and services to its creditors, interest and debt repayment to its bank and salaries to its employees. There are indirect costs associated with financial distress which have a negative impact on the firm's cash flows. For example, managers and employees may demand higher salaries, suppliers may be cautious to enter into long-term contracts and customers may place less value on the service agreements and warranties. Banks may tighten the conditions for loans and may demand a higher markup.

Hedging interest rate risk can reduce the costs related to financial distress. The less a firm can meet its financial obligations and the higher the volatility of its income, the higher the probability of financial distress. Hedging can reduce the volatility of the income and as a result reduce the likelihood that a firm will get into financial distress. Consequently, the costs of financial distress are avoided.

Bankruptcy costs

In contrast to the indirect costs of financial distress, bankruptcy costs are direct costs. These include fees of auditors, legal fees and management fees. Hedging reduces the volatility of the cash flows, reducing the probability of the firm going bankrupt. As a result bankruptcy costs are avoided.

Loss of the debt tax shield

The debt tax shield implies that firms can deduct interest costs from their earnings. As a result pre-tax income and taxes are lower. Also, post-tax income and firm value are higher. From this perspective, firms prefer to use as much debt in their capital structure as possible. Owing to the lower likelihood of getting into financial distress through hedging, firms can take on more debt and can benefit from a higher debt tax shield. As a result, the profit after tax increases and the value of the firm is higher. In this respect the advantages of hedging from a tax perspective and from a financial distress perspective are related.

REDUCING AGENCY COSTS

The third reason for hedging interest rate risk is to reduce agency costs. Fundamentally, a firm is a series of contracts between various parties which have a claim on the same object. These parties try to maximise their individual utility within the limits of their contracts. Agency problems arise from a conflict of interest and through asymmetry in information between shareholders, debt holders and the managers of a firm. Principal–agent issues can also occur between an employer (principal) and an employee (agent) or between shareholders (principal) and the board of directors (agent). This is because asymmetry in information and interests may induce behaviour by the agent which benefits himself but harms the principal.

There are three types of agency costs:

1. Monitoring costs that arise from efforts by the principal to obtain additional information in order to reduce the information asymmetry.
2. Bonding costs that arise from the efforts of the agent to reduce the asymmetry in information.

3. Residual costs, other than those caused by monitoring or bonding.

Moral hazard agency problems between shareholders and debt holders are related to the debt capacity of the firm. A moral hazard agency problem arises if the principal and the agent have the same information before a contract is signed, but after signing the agent has access to superior information compared to the principal. This agency conflict results from the different claims the shareholders and debt holders have on the firm. Whereas debt holders hold fixed claims and bear most of the downside risk, shareholders hold residual claims that are equivalent to a call option on the value of the firm, with the face value of the firm's debt as the option's strike price, and benefit from the upside potential.

Moral hazard agency problems

We discuss two moral hazard agency problems between shareholders and debt holders that concern investment distortions due to debt financing:

- The underinvestment problem
- The asset substitution problem

Underinvestment due to moral hazard agency problems

The optimal investment policy is to accept all positive net present value (NPV) projects and to reject all negative NPV projects. However, if the firm is highly leveraged and the value of its assets is low, managers who are operating in the interest of the shareholders have an incentive to avoid positive NPV projects because the benefits will to a large extent accrue to the debt holders.

Hedging can reduce agency costs. It can reduce the volatility of the income, thereby reducing the risk that the firm cannot meet its interest and debt repayment obligations. As a result, shareholders are less inclined to avoid positive NPV projects and debt holders will not require compensation to protect themselves from underinvestment. Both create firm value. Moreover, by reducing the chance of financial distress, hedging also leads to a more optimal level of debt in the capital structure.

The asset substitution problem

Debt holders require compensation based on the level of risk of the activities of the firm prior to entering into a debt contract.

However, after the debt contract is initialised, shareholders can expropriate wealth from the debt holders by substituting the current assets for more risky assets. Particularly if the firm is close to default, shareholders will have the largest incentive to invest in higher risk projects because as potential gains of the more risky assets accrue to the shareholders, downward risk lies partially with the debt holders. Furthermore, shareholders can directly transfer wealth from debt holders to shareholders through a strong increase in dividends or by issuing more senior debt.

By hedging, firms can alleviate the differences in information and interests between the shareholders and the debt holders. For instance, the firm can commit to a hedging programme over the life of the debt contract prior to its initialisation. This reduces the likelihood of default under the debt obligations. Due to the hedging programme and the resulting lower default risk the shareholders may have less incentive to invest in riskier assets after the debt initialisation. In turn, debt holders will recognise this and will demand less compensation.

Underinvestment due to liquidity limitations

The previous two agency problems between shareholders and debt holders concern underinvestment problems due to debt financing. There are also possible underinvestment problems due to liquidity limitations. The core of the problem is that external financing is more expensive than internal financing. This is due to transaction and agency costs. Transaction costs are costs arising from the issue of new equity or loan capital. Agency costs occur due to asymmetric information before entering into contracts. This relates to an adverse selection principal–agent problem. The theory is that if a firm issues new equity, managers who are acting in the interest of existing shareholders have superior information over new shareholders and tend to issue equity when it is overpriced. New shareholders will anticipate this, leading to a reduction in market prices.

In view of transaction and agency costs, managers prefer internally generated cash flows over expensive external financing. However, internally generated funds can be volatile. This can mean that internal cash flows are insufficient to realise all positive NPV projects. This leads to underinvestment because external financing would increase the cost of capital and decrease the NPV of a project. By reducing the volatility of the cash flows, hedging can increase the possibility that there are sufficient internal funds available for positive NPV projects, reducing the underinvestment problem and increasing firm value.

Hedging can also increase agency costs

Up to now I have discussed how hedging can reduce agency costs. However, hedging can also increase agency costs: while hedging decreases the liquidity-related underinvestment problem, it simultaneously aggravates the overinvestment problem. Hedging can increase the agency conflict between managers and shareholders in the following way: hedging increases the internal funds available at the discretion of managers, which leads to two problems. First, managers may be tempted to use the free cash flow for their personal interests and not in the interests of the shareholders, for instance by growing the company. Firm growth increases the power of the managers as they have more resources under their control and also increases their perquisites, even if they invest in negative NPV projects. Second, as hedging creates internal funds, managers can bypass the monitoring function of the financial markets.

CONTROLLING MANAGERIALISM

The final reason for hedging interest rate risk is to control managerialism and the professionalism of managers.

Managerialism

Managerialism means that self-interested managers may act in their own interest, attempting to maximise their own utility. This relates to contracting problems between managers and shareholders and to information problems between managers and outsiders to the firm. The wealth of managers that is invested in the firm and the managerial compensation can influence hedging decisions. The theory is that hedging policies are derived from the fact that managers maximise their expected lifetime utility. It assumes that managers make hedging decisions according to their compensation.

The form of the management compensation contract can therefore influence the firm's investment decisions.

Example

Management compensation's influence on investment decisions

Porsche's CEO Wendelin Wiedeking received a bonus of 0.9% of Porsche's profits. He led Porsche over a period of 17 years and in his last years, as a result of speculation with option contracts, he is said to have received between €50 and €80 million in remuneration. Since he speculated with the money of the owners of the firm, financially he had a lot to gain and little to lose. This may partly explain the enormous risks he took.

Managers choose a hedging policy for the company that maximises their personal capital. However, by selecting the way in which managers are remunerated shareholders can influence the hedging behaviour of managers so as to align the interests of the managers and the shareholders. There are four forms of remuneration of managers and their corresponding hedging policy:

1. Managers whose remuneration is a concave function of firm value have an incentive to reduce the cash flow variability of the firm and therefore will prefer to hedge less.
2. Managers whose remuneration is based on the share price, or managers who own a significant part of the firm, will have a preference for more hedging, because the manager's wealth is a linear function of firm value.
3. Managers who are remunerated with options prefer to hedge less, because options offer a convex return.
4. Managers with remuneration based on accounting earnings, such as a bonus if the accounting earnings exceed a certain level, will prefer to hedge less because payment is a convex function of the accounting earnings.

Professionalism

Hedging can be a way for firms to demonstrate their entrepreneurial qualities as hedging eliminates extraneous noise, thereby improving the informativeness of corporate earnings. Interest rate risk is outside the sphere of influence of the management of the firm. Through hedging the firm's exposure to interest rate risk the transparency of the firm's performance in its core activities will signal the quality of the management, thereby enhancing its reputation. On the other hand, managers can also deliberately refrain from hedging in order to introduce noise in the corporate earnings.

Part 5

SELECTING THE BEST POSSIBLE DERIVATIVE

INTRODUCTION TO PART 5

Part 5 will examine which derivatives a firm can use to mitigate the effects of interest rate risk on the firm.

Part 5 is the final stage in a firm's interest rate risk management process and builds on the creation of firm value discussed in Part 4: only if hedging makes sense should a firm look at the best possible derivative to mitigate interest rate risk.

Once a firm is exposed to interest rate risk, there are few ways to manage it other than by using derivatives. Part 5 will show you what derivatives a firm can use and how they work. But, even more importantly, I'll also point out exactly where the firm can go wrong when it uses interest rate derivatives. So Part 5 is closely linked to Part 1 where derivatives blunders are analysed. It is essential that you thoroughly grasp the workings and the risks of the derivatives discussed here so that you will be able to understand Part 6, where you'll learn how to establish an optimal interest rate risk strategy.

We'll focus on OTC (over-the-counter) derivatives that are contracted bilaterally between the firm and the bank, unlike exchange-traded derivatives. The reason is that most often firms use OTC derivatives as they can be fully tailored to the requirements of the firm while exchange-traded derivatives have fixed features.

Probably the most used OTC derivatives by firms are interest rate swaps and caps. Nevertheless, I'll discuss a broader range of derivatives so that you are aware of which derivative can be used to mitigate what source of exposure. Each type of derivative will be illustrated.

7

Interest rate derivatives

INTRODUCTION

Derivatives are financial instruments whose value is derived from the value of an underlying asset. In the case of interest rate derivatives, money market and capital market rates are the underlying assets (see Chapter 4). A firm can use interest rate derivatives to hedge risk (decrease risk) or to speculate (increase risk). I assume that derivatives are used to mitigate risk.

There are various types of interest rate derivatives. Basically, they can be broken down into linear derivatives and options, and into OTC and exchange-traded instruments. The schedule below provides an overview of the most important derivatives.

Figure 7.1

The most important derivatives

	Linear derivatives	Options
Exchange-traded	Futures	Options
OTC	Swap FRA	Cap Floor Collar Swaption

This chapter will discuss exchange-traded versus OTC derivatives and linear derivatives versus options. It will also provide you with a graphical overview of which derivative can be used to mitigate which source of exposure to interest rate risk.

EXCHANGE-TRADED VERSUS OTC

A firm can hedge interest rate risk by using exchange-traded derivatives such as futures and options. A future is a standardised contract that is traded at an exchange. It is a forward contract in which parties agree to buy or sell an exchange-traded asset at a fixed date in the future and against a fixed price. An exchange-traded option provides the right to buy or sell bonds within a specific period.

An advantage for firms is that the profit or loss on a futures position is settled by the exchange on a daily basis through margin calls. As a result counterparty risk is limited. Nevertheless, only a limited number of firms use exchange-traded futures and options because the fixed terms and conditions don't provide enough flexibility.

As this book focuses on the perspective of the firm, I'll concentrate on OTC derivatives. These are privately traded between a firm and its bank and are tailored to the specifications required by the firm.

LINEAR DERIVATIVES VERSUS OPTIONS

Linear derivatives are instruments that fix the interest rate. They are like forward contracts: parties agree on settling the difference between an agreed interest rate and the prevailing market interest rate in the future. Interest rate swaps and FRAs (forward rate agreements) are the core linear derivatives. The cost of the derivative is incorporated by the bank in the interest payable or receivable by the firm. The drawback of linear derivatives is that a firm can no longer benefit from favourable interest rate movements, which is a major difference with options.

Options are used to mitigate a negative interest rate movement from the perspective of the firm, while leaving open the chance to benefit from favourable market interest rate movements. Parties agree that the difference between an agreed interest rate and the prevailing market interest rate in the future will only be settled when specific conditions are met. For purchasing options a firm pays an option premium. The most used options by firms are caps. Other commonly used options by firms are collars and swaptions.

SOURCES OF EXPOSURE AND MATCHING DERIVATIVES

So that we can discuss the working of each type of interest derivative in Chapters 8 and 9, there follows an overview of what sources of exposure can be managed with which derivative.

The four sources of interest rate exposure, which are based on the interest-bearing assets and liabilities in the balance sheet, are discussed in Chapter 2: long-term loans, short-term loans, cash and cash equivalents and financial non-current assets. The derivatives that will be discussed in Chapter 8 are swaps and FRAs. The derivatives that will be discussed in Chapter 9 are caps, floors, collars and swaptions. The overview below illustrates the derivatives that can be used to hedge a specific source of interest rate exposure. For instance, short- and long-term loans can be hedged with a payer's swap, while cash and cash equivalents and financial non-current assets can be hedged with a receiver's swap. Short- and long-term loans, for instance, cannot be hedged by selling an FRA.

As this book is about establishing an optimal interest rate risk strategy, which implies decreasing risk, the focus is only on the combinations of sources of exposure and derivatives that mitigate risk.

Figure 7.2

Balance sheet

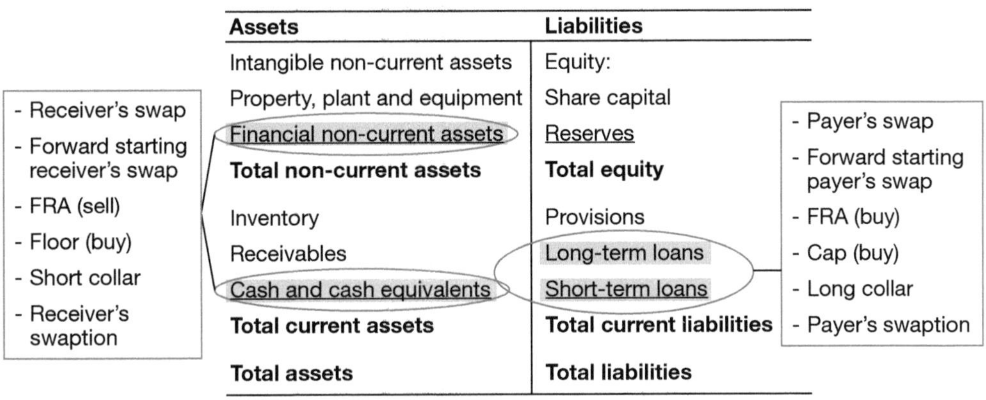

Interest-bearing positions are highlighted.

8

Linear derivatives

INTRODUCTION

Firms can use interest rate swaps and FRAs to mitigate interest rate risk. These derivatives exchange a variable for a fixed interest cash flow stream or vice versa.

The worldwide OTC market for swaps and FRAs is massive. Table 8.1 shows the notional amounts outstanding in billions of US dollars![1] Be aware that all counterparties are incorporated in the figures, including financial institutions.

Table 8.1

Notional amounts outstanding

Notional amounts of swaps and FRAs in US$ billions	December 2011	December 2012	December 2013
Maturity of one year or less	185,644	177,677	184,217
Maturity between 1 and 5 years	154,071	158,028	211,839
Maturity over 5 years	113,492	105,650	139,044
Total	**453,206**	**441,355**	**535,099**

We'll discuss two types of linear interest rate derivatives: interest rate swaps and FRAs. Interest rate swaps can be split into payer's and receiver's swaps. We'll discuss each separately. We will also examine the general workings of a forward starting swap, which is a payer's or receiver's swap that starts in the future. The last part about interest rate swaps shows you how interest rate swaps are valued. Finally, we'll go into FRAs.

INTEREST RATE SWAP

In the case of an interest rate swap two parties agree to exchange interest cash flows from a variable rate to a fixed rate or vice versa. One party pays the fixed interest rate (the swap rate) to the other party during the lifetime of the swap. The counterparty pays the variable (also called floating) interest rate: a reference rate such as LIBOR or Euribor. The cash flow streams of a swap are called legs. Swaps have two legs: a fixed and a variable leg.

Interest cash flows in swaps can be exchanged in the same currency or in different currencies. If the exchange of interest cash flows is in different currencies, it is called a cross currency interest rate swap. With a swap in the same currency the underlying notional principal amount on which the interest calculations are based is not exchanged. In contrast, with cross currency interest rate swaps the notional principal amount is usually exchanged. I will focus here on swaps with cash flows in the same currency.

The main specifications of an interest rate swap are usually those shown in Table 8.2.

Table 8.2 **Main specifications of an interest rate swap**

Contract term:	Agreed between the buyer and the seller
Notional principal amount:	Agreed between the buyer and the seller
Fixed leg	
Contract rate:	Swap rate
Day count:	30 / 360 (capital market convention)
Payment:	Semi-annually or annually
Variable leg	
Reference rate:	3- or 6-months money market rate such as Euribor or LIBOR
Day count:	Actual number of days / 360* (money market convention)
Payment:	Quarterly or semi-annually

*365 for GBP

A swap can be tailored to the specific demands of a firm. For instance, the notional principal amount of the swap can be decreased during its life to match the principal of the underlying interest-bearing asset or liability.

Key issues of derivatives blunders From the derivatives blunders in Part 1 we have learned that a major risk with swaps is a mismatch in the notional principal amount or in the term between the derivative and the underlying exposure. Therefore, be aware of the

- Materialisation of the underlying exposure
- Debt schedule of the underlying load
- Possible early repayment of the underlying loan

There are various types of interest rate swaps:

- Payer's swaps
- Receiver's swaps
- Forward starting payer's and receiver's swaps

The terms payer and receiver relate to the party paying the fixed interest rate: the party buying a payer's swap pays the fixed interest rate while receiving the variable interest rate. The counterparty automatically sells a receiver's swap paying the variable interest rate and receiving the fixed interest rate. Payer's and receiver's swaps are therefore the two sides of the same coin.

Payer's swap

A firm can use a payer's swap to mitigate interest rate risk of short- and long-term loans.

Figure 8.1

Balance sheet

Assets	Liabilities	
Intangible non-current assets	Equity:	
Property, plant and equipment	Share capital	
Financial non-current assets	Reserves	
Total non-current assets	**Total equity**	
Inventory	Provisions	
Receivables	Long-term loans	Payer's swap
Cash and cash equivalents	Short-term loans	Payer's swap
Total current assets	**Total current liabilities**	
Total assets	**Total liabilities**	

Interest-bearing positions are highlighted.

Example

Payer's swap

A firm has a variable interest rate loan. Interest payable is based on 3-months GBP LIBOR and a markup of 1.5%. The firm purchases a payer's swap. As a result it will pay the fixed rate (5%) and receive the variable rate. The figures below show the interest cash flows that occur before and after the swap. ▶

Before the swap

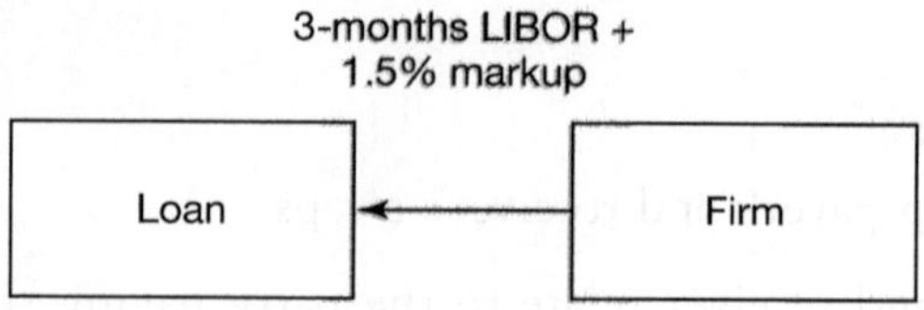

After the swap

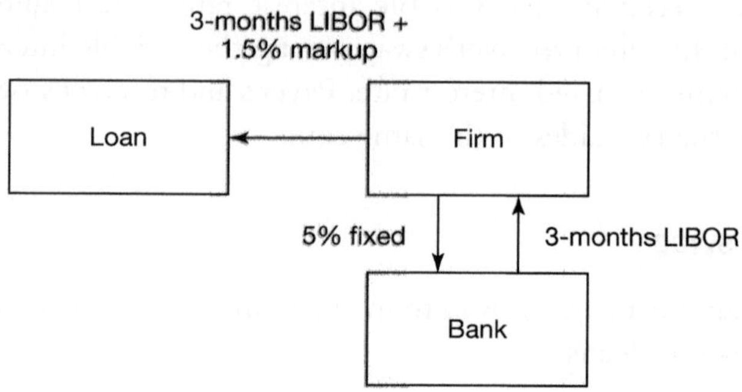

Result

Interest payable by the firm before the swap

Interest payable:	3-months LIBOR + 1.5% markup

Interest payable by the firm after the swap

Interest payable:	5% fixed
Interest payable:	3-months LIBOR + 1.5% markup
Interest receivable:	3-months LIBOR
Net interest payable:	5% fixed + 1.5% markup

Ultimately, through entering into a payer's swap the firm pays the fixed rate of 5% and the markup of 1.5% as 3-months GBP LIBOR is both paid and received.

> From Part 1 we know that a common error is to assume that with a payer's swap interest payable is fully fixed. This is not the case because the markup can be adjusted by the bank.

The figure below presents the interest payable by the firm with and without the payer's swap. The markup is not included. It shows that, after entering into a payer's swap, interest payable (excluding markup) is not affected by market interest rate movements.

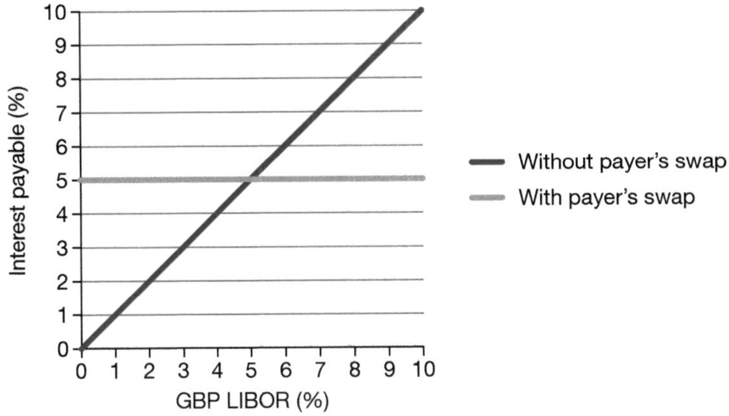

Receiver's swap

A firm can use a receiver's swap to mitigate interest rate risk of cash and cash equivalents and financial non-current assets.

Figure 8.2

Balance sheet

- Receiver's swap

Assets	**Liabilities**
Intangible non-current assets	Equity:
Property, plant and equipment	Share capital
Financial non-current assets	Reserves
Total non-current assets	**Total equity**
Inventory	Provisions
Receivables	Long-term loans
Cash and cash equivalents	Short-term loans
Total current assets	**Total current liabilities**
Total assets	**Total liabilities**

Interest-bearing positions are highlighted.

Example

Receiver's swap

A firm has lent money to a third party (financial non-current assets) against 3-months Euribor + 2% markup. The loan has a remaining life of 4 years. The 4-year swap rate is 4%. The firm purchases a receiver's swap. The figure below shows the interest flows before and after buying the receiver's swap.

Before the swap

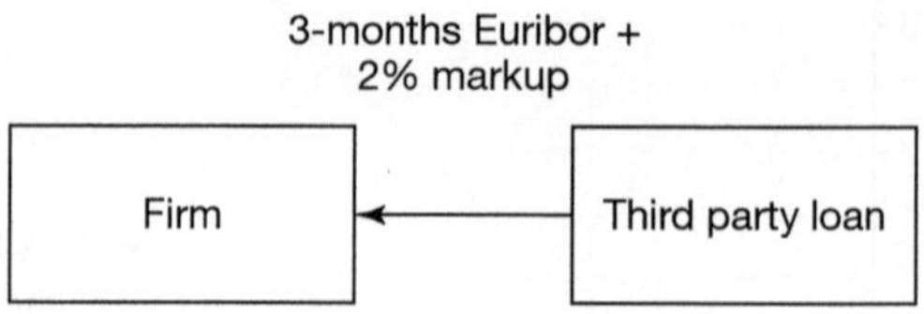

After the swap

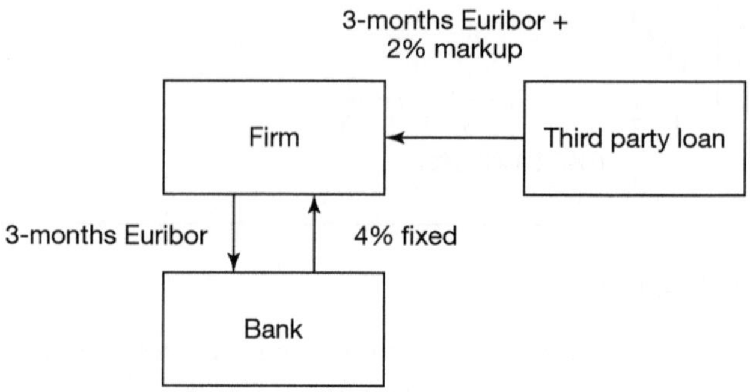

Result

<u>Interest receivable before the swap</u>

Interest receivable:	Euribor + 2% markup

<u>Interest receivable after the swap</u>

Interest receivable:	3-months Euribor + 2% markup
Interest receivable:	4% fixed
Interest payable:	<u>3-months Euribor</u>
Net interest receivable:	4% fixed + 2% markup

Ultimately, through entering into a receiver's swap the firm receives 4% fixed + 2% markup. If the firm doesn't change the markup during the life of the swap, it receives 6% fixed.

As with payer's swaps a major risk with receiver's swaps is a mismatch in the notional principal amount or in the term between the derivative and the underlying exposure. In this particular case the firm should be aware of:

- Problems of the third party to meet its interest and debt redemption payments
- Possible early repayment of the loan by the third party

Forward starting payer's and receiver's swap

A forward starting swap is a contract to exchange a variable rate for a fixed rate in the future or vice versa. The future interest rate is already fixed in advance.

The specifications of a forward starting swap are to a large extent similar to a regular interest rate swap, except for the forward starting date of the swap. The fixed interest depends on the forward interest rates, which are based on the yield curve at the moment of inception of the swap. In the case of a normal yield curve the forward rates are higher than the current rates. This difference increases with the steepness of the yield curve. In the case of a flat or inversed yield curve the forward rates will respectively be more or less the same or lower than the current rates.

> The risks of a forward starting swap are similar to those mentioned for regular swaps. Nevertheless, as forward starting swaps are mostly used to manage a future underlying exposure, the risk of the expected exposure not materialising is a notable risk with this type of derivative.

Valuation of swaps

At the inception of a swap, the value of its fixed rate cash flows are equal to the expected value of the variable rate cash flows implied by the forward curve of the reference money market rate. Therefore, at the start of a swap it has a net present value of zero, except for the margin of the bank. During the lifetime of the swap, its value can change as a function of the difference between the present value of the future cash inflows minus the present value of the future cash outflows.

As I mentioned before, with a swap that has both legs in the same currency there is no exchange of the notional principal amount. However, for calculating the market value of a swap it can be assumed that at maturity the notional principal amount is exchanged bilaterally. From the point of view of a firm that has purchased a payer's swap, the swap can then be seen as a combination of two opposite loans that can be valued separately:

- A fixed rate loan
- A variable rate investment

The advantage of this approach is that the present value is more easily determined. The value of the fixed rate loan is established by calculating the present value of the remaining cash flows: these are certain upfront. When the actual swap rate is higher (lower) than the fixed rate of the swap, the value of the loan is lower (higher) than its nominal value. The value of the variable rate investment is more difficult to establish because future interest rates and the corresponding cash flows are variable and are not yet certain. However, because the variable interest received is relatively quickly adjusted to the money market rate due to the short term (most variable legs are based on a 3- or 6-month money market reference rate), in practice there will be no large difference between the reference rate and the prevailing variable rate and the value of the variable rate investment will be close to 100%.

This indicates that the value of a swap is primarily determined by the difference between the fixed interest of the swap and the actual swap rate. From the perspective of the firm, if the actual swap rate is lower (higher) than the fixed rate of the swap, the value of a payer's swap will be negative (positive).

Hence, the development of the value of a payer's swap can be compared to that of a fixed rate loan: when the market rate decreases since a firm has financed with a fixed rate loan, the firm will have to pay a penalty interest fee in case of early termination.

In the case of early termination a significant difference between a payer's swap and a fixed rate loan is that when the market rate is higher than the fixed interest on the swap, the firm with the swap receives the positive market value whereas with the fixed rate loan the firm does not receive any compensation at all.

The value of a forward starting swap is derived in the same manner as that of a standard swap. An important given is that the value of a forward starting swap is already subject to value changes of the underlying interest rates from its inception. If the firm does not want to use the forward starting swap, for example because the underlying investment did not materialise, it has to unwind the swap, which can lead to a settlement of a positive or negative market value.

FRA

A firm can use an FRA to mitigate interest rate risk of all interest-bearing assets and liabilities.

Figure 8.3

Balance sheet

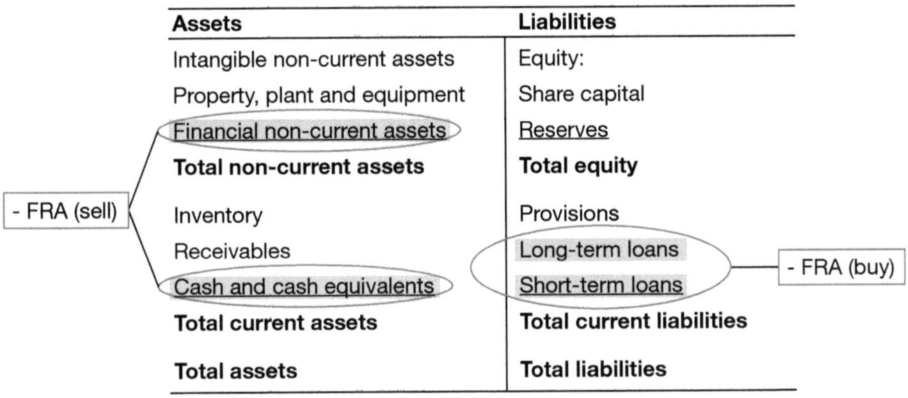

Interest-bearing positions are highlighted.

An FRA resembles an interest rate swap as it fixes a future interest rate. It is a contract between two parties to determine the rate of interest to be paid or received over a notional principal amount at a future start date. A firm buying an FRA locks in a reference money market rate in order to protect itself from an interest rate increase, while a firm selling an FRA protects itself from an interest rate decrease. Only the difference between the contract rate and the prevailing money market rate is exchanged at settlement. A firm that buys an FRA is compensated by the seller if the reference rate is higher than the contract rate and vice versa.

Basically, an interest rate swap can be seen as a chain of FRAs on the basis of one fixed interest rate. The main difference is that with an FRA settlement is only made once. Furthermore, the timing of the settlement differs between a swap and an FRA: whereas settlement with a swap is at the end of the period, settlement with an FRA is at the beginning of the underlying period because the present value of the amount to be settled is already known at that moment.

Cash flows from FRAs generally don't perfectly match those of the underlying interest-bearing positions as the latter usually generate cash flows at the end of an interest rate period.

The notation of an FRA is for instance 1×4. This implies that the FRA starts one month from now. The maturity date is four months from now. The underlying rate can be derived by subtracting the start date from the maturity date: in this case the underlying rate is the 3-month money market rate. A quote of 2.01/2.03% indicates that a firm that buys an FRA pays the fixed rate of 2.03% and receives the variable 3-month rate, while a firm that sells an FRA pays the variable 3-month rate and receives the fixed rate of 2.01%.

The money market convention for the interest calculations is generally the actual number of days divided by 360. Only for GBP the actual number of days is divided by 365.

Example

FRA

A firm will complete a project in a few years' time. Payments from the customer are at the end of the project. The firm is financed on the basis of GBP LIBOR + 1% markup. It can deposit surplus cash for GBP LIBOR – 0.25%. The estimated cash position is:

Month 3–Month 6	£10 million deficit
Month 6–Month 9	£15 million deficit
Month 9–Month 12	£20 million deficit
Month 12–Month 24	£5 million surplus

Up to Month 12 there is a cash shortage and the firm will draw under the financing facility. The risk for the firm is that the money market rate increases, as a result of which interest payable will increase. From Month 12 there is a cash surplus. The risk for the firm then is that the money market rate decreases and as a result interest receivable from the future deposits will decrease. The firm can eliminate interest rate risk by using FRAs.

The FRA rates:

Period	Rate	Period	Rate
1×4	2.01–2.03%	1×7	2.16–2.18%
2×5	2.10–2.12%	2×8	2.26–2.28%
3×6	2.20–2.22%	3×9	2.34–2.36%
4×7	2.28–2.30%	4×10	2.42–2.44%
5×8	2.37–2.39%	5×11	2.47–2.49%
6×9	2.43–2.45%	6×12	2.53–2.55%
9×12	2.60–2.62%	12×18	2.73–2.75%
12×24	2.82–2.84%	18×24	2.90–2.92%

The firm enters into the following FRAs:

Buy	£10 million	3×6	2.22%
	£15 million	6×9	2.45%
	£20 million	9×12	2.62%
Sell	£5 million	12×24	2.82%

Effects of the FRA with an increasing GBP LIBOR rate:

Date	Prevailing GBP LIBOR rate	FRA contract rate	Interest settlement	Loan / deposit	Total interest payable / receivable
Month 3	2.30%	2.22%	0.08%	3.30%	3.22%
Month 6	2.60%	2.45%	0.15%	3.60%	3.45%
Month 9	2.75%	2.62%	0.13%	3.75%	3.62%
Month 12	2.90%	2.82%	0.08%	2.65%	2.57%

As an alternative, the firm could also have mitigated interest rate risk by entering into a fixed rate financing of £20 million and by placing surplus cash on deposit. However, this would have resulted in a loss due to the bank's margins (GBP LIBOR + 1% versus GBP LIBOR – 0.25%).

9

Options

INTRODUCTION

In this chapter I analyse the use of options for managing interest rate risk. The advantage for a firm of using an option versus a linear derivative is that while both mitigate interest rate risk, only options provide the possibility of benefiting from favourable market rate movements. This is in contrast to linear derivatives. The drawback is that the firm has to pay an option premium. The option premium is seen as interest and is recorded in the interest line item of the income statement and the cash flow statement.

There are various types of options. The basic forms are the cap (maximises interest payable) and the floor (minimises interest receivable). The reference rate is maximised or minimised: this is called the strike price of the option. You can buy or sell options. By buying options interest rate risk is decreased. By selling options interest rate risk is increased.

In the case of buying an option, the firm has the right but not the obligation to exercise the option. In the case of selling an option, the firm has the obligation to deliver. In return an option premium is received. A collar is a combination of buying a cap and selling a floor or vice versa. Table 9.1 summarises the effects of options.

Table 9.1 **The effects of options**

Type	Effect
Cap	Maximises interest payable
Floor	Minimises interest receivable
Collar	Creates a range for interest payable or receivable

The worldwide OTC market for options is smaller than that for swaps and FRAs. Table 9.2 shows the notional amounts outstanding in billions of US dollars.[1] All types of counterparties feature in the figures, including financial institutions.

Table 9.2 **Amounts outstanding in US$ bn**

Notional amounts of OTC options in US$ billions	December 2011	December 2012	December 2013
Maturity of 1 year or less	13,719	12,995	14,085
Maturity between 1 and 5 years	22,350	22,234	22,446
Maturity over 5 years	14,842	13,122	12,734
Total	**50,911**	**48,351**	**49,264**

Key issues of derivatives blunders Considering the derivatives blunders discussed in Part 1, firms can avoid certain blunders by using options instead of swaps:

- Negative value of derivatives: when a firm buys an option, there is no negative value of the derivative as during its life an option has either a positive value or a value of nil.
- Link between derivative and underlying loan: if a firm buys an option, the option premium is due upfront. As a result the bank does not run credit risk on the firm.* Thus, the firm will have no problem in changing banks from this point of view
- Overhedging with derivatives: this does not create a risk when a firm buys an option because the firm has purchased a right and not an obligation.

*The firm does run credit risk on the bank if the option has a positive value.

We'll discuss the following four types of options. The overview presented with each type shows which source of exposure to interest rate risk can be hedged by that specific option.

- Cap
- Floor
- Collar
- Swaption

CAP

A firm can buy a cap to protect its short- and long-term loans against an increase of the money market rate, while at the same time benefiting from a money market decrease.

Figure 9.1

Balance sheet

Assets	Liabilities
Intangible non-current assets	Equity:
Property, plant and equipment	Share capital
Financial non-current assets	Reserves
Total non-current assets	**Total equity**
Inventory	Provisions
Receivables	Long-term loans — Cap (buy)
Cash and cash equivalents	Short-term loans — Cap (buy)
Total current assets	**Total current liabilities**
Total assets	**Total liabilities**

Interest-bearing positions are highlighted.

A cap is an option that protects the buyer against an increase of the money market rate. The seller of a cap is obliged, if the money market rate at previously determined dates is higher than the strike price, to pay the difference to the buyer. The buyer pays an option premium for the protection, yet can still benefit from future money market rate decreases. The option premium is usually paid upfront.

The common specifications for a cap are shown in Table 9.3.

Table 9.3

Specifications for a cap

Contract term:	To be agreed between the buyer and the seller
Notional principal amount:	To be agreed between the buyer and the seller
Reference rate:	3-, 6- or 12-months money market rate such as Euribor or LIBOR
Day count:	Actual number of days / 360* (money market convention)
Strike price:	To be agreed between the buyer and the seller
Option premium:	Depending on market circumstances

*365 for GBP

The frequency of the expiration dates is determined by the chosen reference rate (e.g. 3 or 6 months). The reference rate determines the dates of interest settlement. Often the reference rate is Euribor or LIBOR. At every new interest rate period the reference rate is compared to the prevailing money market rate: the difference is settled at the end of each interest rate period. Because the reference rate is usually known at the start of the contract, the first period is often disregarded.

Example

Cap

A firm has a loan of $10 million. The term is 7 years. Interest is based on 3-months USD LIBOR and a markup of 1%. The firm purchases a cap and pays the option premium at the start of the option contract. Spread out over the total life of the cap the premium is 0.40% per year.

Principal:	$10 million
Term:	7 years
Markup:	1% yearly (may change over the life of the loan)
Cap strike:	3%
Reference rate:	3-months USD LIBOR
Premium:	0.40% yearly

Table 9.4 shows the effect of the cap at different USD LIBOR levels.

Table 9.4

USD LIBOR	Strike price	Settlement	Option premium	Markup	Total interest payable with cap	Total interest payable without cap
1%	3%	0%	0.40%	1.00%	2.40%	2.00%
2%	3%	0%	0.40%	1.00%	3.40%	3.00%
3%	3%	0%	0.40%	1.00%	4.40%	4.00%
4%	3%	1%	0.40%	1.00%	4.40%	5.00%
5%	3%	2%	0.40%	1.00%	4.40%	6.00%
6%	3%	3%	0.40%	1.00%	4.40%	7.00%
7%	3%	4%	0.40%	1.00%	4.40%	8.00%
8%	3%	5%	0.40%	1.00%	4.40%	9.00%

As a result of the cap, interest payable by the firm is maximised at 4.40% (i.e. the sum of the strike price, the option premium and the markup).

Table 9.4 presents the interest payable by the firm with and without cap.

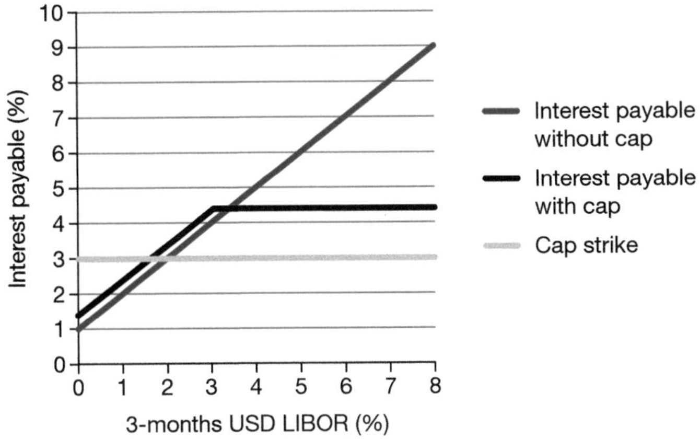

The figure shows that up to a 3-months USD LIBOR rate of 3.40% the firm's total interest payable is higher with the cap than without the cap due to the option premium of 0.40%. When the USD LIBOR rate is above 3.40% total interest payable is lower with the cap than without the cap because the cap protects the firm against money market rates above the strike price of 3%.

Valuation of a cap

The value of a cap is estimated by calculating the present value of the interest settlements from the cap and depends on the following factors:

- Term
- Reference rate
- Strike price
- Yield curve
- Interest rate volatility

The estimation of the chance of payment of the cap is important. The longer the term of the cap, the lower the cap strike and the higher the expected volatility of the reference rate, the greater the chance of payment and the higher the option premium will be.

> After buying a cap a firm can close it during its life and receive the positive market value if applicable. Because a cap is a right, in contrast to a two-sided commitment in the case of an interest swap, the value of the cap is either positive or nil and therefore a firm does not run the risk of having to pay a negative value. Thus the maximum lost is the option premium.

FLOOR

A firm can buy a floor to protect its variable interest-bearing assets, such as cash and cash equivalents and financial non-current assets, against a decrease of the money market rate, while at the same time benefiting from a money market increase.

The characteristics of a floor match those of a cap. The primary difference is that a firm that buys a floor is protected against market rate decreases while a firm that buys a cap is protected against market rate increases.

Figure 9.2

Balance sheet

- Floor (buy) → Financial non-current assets; Cash and cash equivalents

Assets	Liabilities
Intangible non-current assets	Equity:
Property, plant and equipment	Share capital
Financial non-current assets	Reserves
Total non-current assets	**Total equity**
Inventory	Provisions
Receivables	Long-term loans
Cash and cash equivalents	Short-term loans
Total current assets	**Total current liabilities**
Total assets	**Total liabilities**

Interest-bearing positions are highlighted.

Example

Floor

A firm invests £5 million in 3-month deposits. Each period these deposits are renewed. Interest receivable by the firm is GBP LIBOR minus 0.30%. The firm purchases a floor to protect the yields against a lower future GBP LIBOR rate. Spread over a period of a year, the option premium is 0.50%.

Notional principal amount:	£5 million
Contract term:	5 years
Floor strike:	4.00%
Reference rate:	3-months GBP LIBOR
Option premium:	0.50 yearly
Margin deposit:	0.30%

Table 9.5 shows the effect of the floor at different GBP LIBOR levels.

Table 9.5

GBP LIBOR	Strike price	Settlement	Option premium	Margin	Total interest receivable with floor	Total interest receivable without floor
1%	4.00%	3%	0.50%	0.30%	3.20%	0.70%
2%	4.00%	2%	0.50%	0.30%	3.20%	1.70%
3%	4.00%	1%	0.50%	0.30%	3.20%	2.70%
4%	4.00%	0%	0.50%	0.30%	3.20%	3.70%
5%	4.00%	0%	0.50%	0.30%	4.20%	4.70%
6%	4.00%	0%	0.50%	0.30%	5.20%	5.70%
7%	4.00%	0%	0.50%	0.30%	6.20%	6.70%
8%	4.00%	0%	0.50%	0.30%	7.20%	7.70%

As a result of the floor, interest receivable by the firm is minimised at 3.20%. The strike of the floor is reduced by the option premium and by the margin.

Figure 9.3 shows a comparison between the firm's total interest receivable, with and without a floor. ▶

Figure 9.3

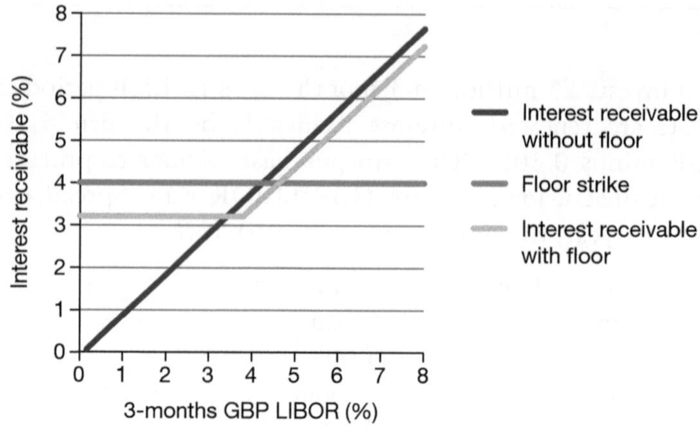

COLLAR

In contrast to a single cap or floor, a firm can use a collar to protect all interest-bearing positions against negative money market movements, while at the same time benefiting from positive movements.

Figure 9.4

Balance sheet

Assets	Liabilities
Intangible non-current assets	Equity:
Property, plant and equipment	Share capital
Financial non-current assets	Reserves
Total non-current assets	**Total equity**
Inventory	Provisions
Receivables	Long-term loans
Cash and cash equivalents	Short-term loans
Total current assets	**Total current liabilities**
Total assets	**Total liabilities**

- Short collar (Financial non-current assets; Cash and cash equivalents)

- Long collar (Long-term loans; Short-term loans)

A collar is a combination of buying a cap and selling a floor (long collar) or the other way round (short collar). In the former case the buyer of a collar maximises interest payable through the cap. In order to lower the option premium of the cap, the firm at the same time sells a floor. As a result of the floor the firm settles for a certain minimum interest payable (the floor strike). With respect to a long collar, there are three possibilities depending on the movement of the money market reference rate:

- If the reference rate is above the cap strike, the seller pays the difference to the buyer.
- If the reference rate is below the floor strike, the buyer pays the difference to the seller.
- If the reference rate is between the cap and the floor strike, no settlement takes place.

The result of a collar is that interest payable remains between a certain range defined by the cap and the floor strike.

When buying a cap and selling a floor a firm can determine the specifications in such a way that both option premiums cancel each other out, resulting into a zero cost collar. With a zero cost collar a firm can for instance protect itself against an interest rate increase without any costs. However, at the same time the firm has limited its benefits from a money market rate decrease. A zero cost strategy consisting of a cap and floor with the same principal and strike price equals an interest rate swap as the position is completely fixed.

Example

Collar

A firm has a loan with a principal of €15 million. The term is 3 years and interest payable is based on 3-months Euribor + 0.75%. The firm buys a cap and sells a floor.

Principal amount:	€15 million
Term:	3 years
Reference rate:	3-months Euribor
Markup:	0.75% (may change over the life of the loan)
Cap strike:	4.00%
Floor strike:	3.00%
Option premium:	€0 (zero cost)

The results of this strategy at different 3-months Euribor rates are now shown in Table 9.6. ▶

Table 9.6

Euribor	Cap strike	Floor strike	Settlement	Markup	Total interest payable with collar	Total interest payable without collar
1%	4.00%	3.00%	-2.00%	0.75%	3.75%	1.75%
2%	4.00%	3.00%	-1.00%	0.75%	3.75%	2.75%
3%	4.00%	3.00%	0.00%	0.75%	3.75%	3.75%
3.5%	4.00%	3.00%	0.00%	0.75%	4.25%	4.25%
4%	4.00%	3.00%	0.00%	0.75%	4.75%	4.75%
5%	4.00%	3.00%	1.00%	0.75%	4.75%	5.75%
6%	4.00%	3.00%	2.00%	0.75%	4.75%	6.75%
7%	4.00%	3.00%	3.00%	0.75%	4.75%	7.75%
8%	4.00%	3.00%	4.00%	0.75%	4.75%	8.75%

As a result of the collar, interest rate payments by the firm are maximised at 4.75% (i.e. the cap strike plus the markup from the loan). The minimum interest payable is 3.75% (i.e. the floor strike plus the markup).

Figure 9.5 shows a comparison between the firm's total interest payable, with and without the collar.

Figure 9.5

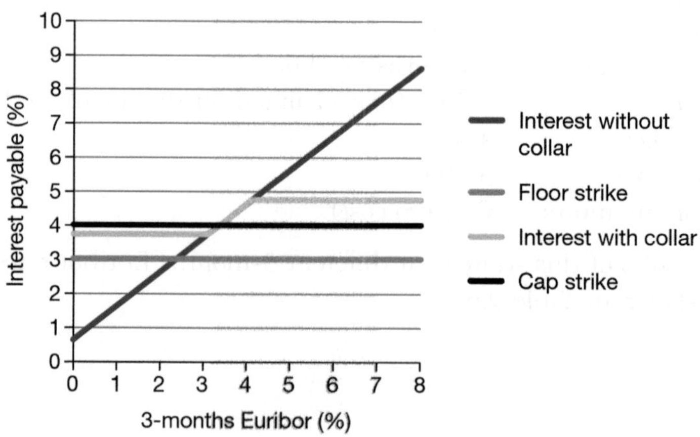

SWAPTION

A firm can use a swaption to mitigate all types of interest-bearing positions that arise in the future against interest rate risk, without the obligation to enter into the swap if the firm does not want to.

Figure 9.6

Balance sheet

Assets	Liabilities
Intangible non-current assets	Equity:
Property, plant and equipment	Share capital
Financial non-current assets	Reserves
Total non-current assets	**Total equity**
Inventory	Provisions
Receivables	Long-term loans
Cash and cash equivalents	Short-term loans
Total current assets	**Total current liabilities**
Total assets	**Total liabilities**

- Receiver's swaption (Financial non-current assets; Cash and cash equivalents)

- Payer's swaption (Long-term loans; Short-term loans)

A swaption is an option on an interest rate swap. As with interest rate swaps there are payer's swaptions and receiver's swaptions. The buyer of a swaption has the right but not the obligation to enter the swap. The buyer of a payer's swaption will exercise this right if the reference rate at expiration is higher than the agreed rate in the swaption. This protects the buyer against an increase of the capital market interest rate, for instance when signing a financing arrangement in the future, while benefiting from a decrease of the capital market rate. In the latter case the option will not be exercised and the buyer loses the option premium paid. The financing can then be arranged at the lower prevailing market rate.

Key issues of derivatives blunders

From the derivatives blunders in Part 1 we've learned that firms sometimes sign interest rate swap contracts before the underlying financing is arranged. If circumstances alter in the intermediate period and the financing doesn't materialise, the result is an open swap position without an underlying interest-bearing liability. By using a swaption, this derivatives blunder can be avoided. If the swaption turns out to be redundant, it can be sold in the case of a positive market value. Of course, the firm has to bear the costs of the option premium.

The difference between a cap and a swaption is that a swaption is one option and a cap is a series of options. Furthermore, a swaption usually has a substantially shorter term than a cap. Also, a cap relates to future money market rates while a swaption concerns a future capital market rate at a specific point in time.

Example

Payer's swaption

A firm has an expected financing need of ¥1 billion over one year. The term of the future variable rate loan (based on 6-months JPY LIBOR) is 7 years. The firm wants to buy a payer's swaption to protect itself against future capital market rate increases and wants to benefit from market rate decreases.

Loan	
Principal loan:	¥1 billion
Term loan:	7 years
Interest rate loan:	6-months JPY LIBOR
Markup loan:	1% (may change over the life of the loan)
Swaption	
Principal swaption:	¥1 billion
Strike price:	3.50%
Term swaption:	1 year
Term swap:	7 years
Reference rate:	6-months JPY LIBOR
Swaption premium:	0.20%

If the 7-year swap rate at expiration of the swaption is higher than 3.50%, the swaption will be exercised and the interest on the loan is fixed at 3.50%. Together with the variable rate loan, the cash flows then are:

Before the swaption

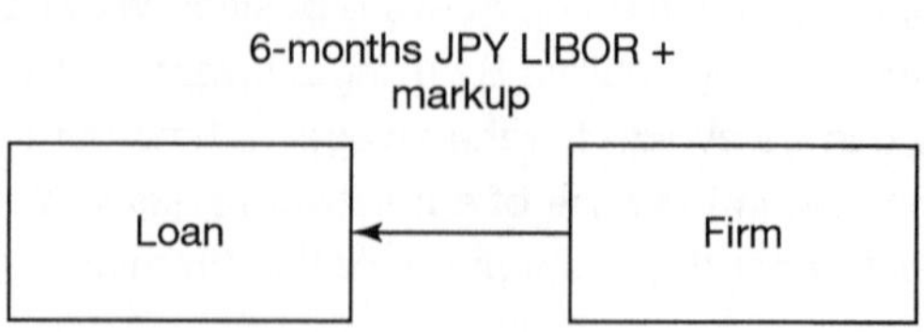

After the swaption

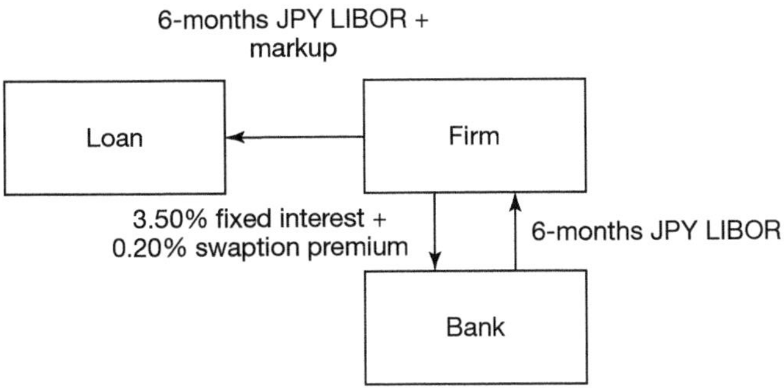

If the 7-year swap rate is lower than 3.50%, the swaption will expire worthless as the interest rate can be fixed at a lower level. However, interest payable by the firm is increased by the swaption premium of 0.20% per year.

Result swaption

Depending on the prevailing 7-year swap rate at expiration of the swap, total interest payable by the firm amounts to either:

7-year swap rate ≤ 3.50:	prevailing capital market rate + markup + 0.20% swaption premium
7-year swap rate > 3.50:	3.50% fixed rate + markup + 0.20% swaption premium

Part 6

HOW TO FORMULATE THE OPTIMAL STRATEGY: THE ANALYTICAL METHOD

INTRODUCTION TO PART 6

Part 6 is the key part of *Mastering Interest Rate Risk Strategy*. The derivatives blunders in Part 1 show us how not to do it. Parts 2 to 5 present the theory behind the natural sequence of a firm's interest rate risk management process. Part 6 shows you how to formulate an optimal strategy for managing corporate interest rate risk. For this purpose I'm going to introduce a proven analytical method called the Macrae RISK Reduction Rules®. In Appendix II you can find information on how the method is proven.

In a step by step approach, the RISK Reduction Rules tie all information from the previous five Parts together. Using them ensures that you:

- Create instead of decrease firm value by hedging interest rate risk
- Formulate a strategy that is optimal to the specific situation of the firm
- Avoid the pitfalls that can lead to derivatives blunders

RISK has four steps and is an acronym that stands for:

I. Risk formulation
II. Impact analysis
III. Scenario analysis
IV. Knowledge application

The goal of Step I is to formulate the right question because the later steps will provide an answer to this question. The goal of Step II is to determine if hedging interest rate risk creates value for the firm. This is important because hedging in itself, such as for instance by using derivatives, does not necessarily create firm value! The goal of Step III is to examine how the interest rate risk of a firm can be hedged and whether there are other, more structural, ways of mitigating risk than by using derivatives. The goal of Step IV is to provide an answer to the risk issue established in Step I.

The RISK method focuses on interest rate risk from a corporate perspective. A corporate is primarily concerned with the effects of interest rate movements in its income and cash flow statement. In contrast, institutional investors, such as pension funds and insurers, have a different focus. They are primarily concerned with the effects of changes in interest rates on the value of their assets and liabilities. For our target group of non-financial firms, the development in value of interest-bearing assets and liabilities is not the main issue.

The strengths of the RISK Reduction Rules are:

- They are academically solid.
- They are proven in practice.
- They are designed to create firm value.
- They are based on the firm's concrete figures.
- They are reproducible.
- They can be used as a commercial tool.

I'll first introduce you to a new financing arrangement for Trader, the central case in this book. Then I'll show you the RISK Reduction Rules in full in order to provide an overview of the whole process. Finally, I'll go through each step of the Rules using Trader as an illustration.

10

The Macrae RISK Reduction Rules®

Central case, Trader: new financing arrangement

The analytical method in full

The analytical method step by step

CENTRAL CASE, TRADER: NEW FINANCING ARRANGEMENT

We introduced the central case, Trader, in Chapter 5 in order to support the analysis of the impact of interest rate risk on the financial statements of the firm. The central case is presented in Appendix I.

Trader negotiates a new financing agreement with its bank, which will take effect on 1 January 2015. The key data of this financing arrangement are presented below.

Trader has two financial covenants in its new financing arrangement:

- Interest Coverage Ratio (ICR) > 3
- Solvency > 25%

Trader wants to ensure that its financial covenants are always met in order to avoid a situation of financial distress. This is an important argument for hedging interest rate risk because Trader is close to breaching its solvency and particularly its ICR ratio. Therefore, the management of Trader wants to develop an optimal strategy to manage interest rate risk with a view to avoiding the breach of one of the financial covenants.

Table 10.1

Overview new financing arrangement

Type of loan	**Principal**
Real estate loan	€21,000,000
Current account overdraft	€48,000,000
GBP term loan	£4,000,000*
Real estate loan	
Principal:	€21,000,000
Purpose:	Financing of real estate
Term:	10 years
Debt redemption:	40 quarterly instalments of €262,500 + final instalment of €10,500,000
Interest payable:	3-months Euribor + 0.90% markup
Calculation method:	Actual days / 360
Drawdown:	Full drawdown of the principal in a lump sum at the start

Current account overdraft

Principal:	€48,000,000
Purpose:	Financing of the working capital needs
Term:	Daily cancellable
Debt redemption:	Not applicable
Debit interest:	1-month Euribor + markup based on pricing grid

The pricing grid is based on the net debt / EBITDA ratio:

5.0 – 6.0	1.00%
4.0 – 5.0	0.90%
< 4.0	0.80%
Calculation method:	Actual days / 360
Drawdown:	Flexible drawdown up to €48 million
Credit interest:	From €0 – €100,000: 0%, above €100,000: variable bank rate (based on Euribor minus a margin)
Calculation method:	Actual days/360

Trader will focus on efficient cash management in order to achieve a lowest possible positive balance on its current account.

GBP term loan

Principal:	£4,000,000
Purpose:	Financing of the working capital needs in British Pounds
Term:	10 years
Debt redemption:	£400,000 yearly
Interest payable:	6-months GBP LIBOR + 1.10% markup
Calculation method:	Actual days / 365
Drawdown:	Full drawdown of the principal in a lump sum at the start

*The functional currency of Trader is the euro.

Trader acknowledges the impact of interest rate risk on the net debt / EBITDA ratio through volatility in interest cash flows. However, Trader believes this to be less important than breaching its financial covenants and therefore our focus is on the latter.

In our analysis of Trader we will focus solely on interest rate risk and not on other risks, such as foreign exchange risk.

THE ANALYTICAL METHOD IN FULL

Below, the RISK Reduction Rules are presented in full.

Formulate the optimal strategy to manage interest rate risk

Figure 10.1

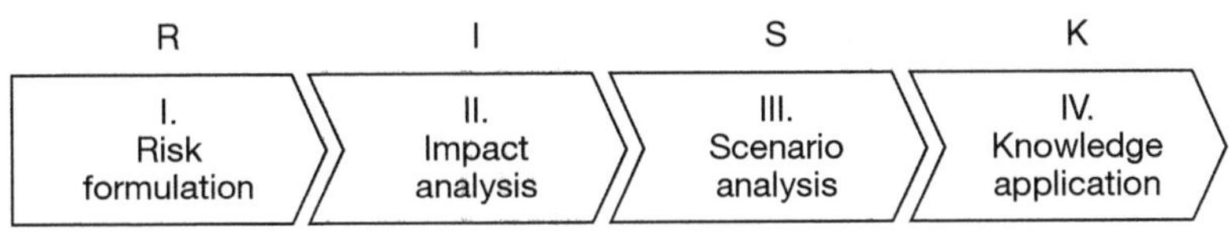

THE ANALYTICAL METHOD STEP BY STEP

I will now go through the RISK Reduction Rules step by step. First, each of the four steps is presented graphically. Then they are explained in detail.

THE MACRAE RISK REDUCTION RULES®

Step I. Risk formulation

I. Risk formulation

Figure 10.2

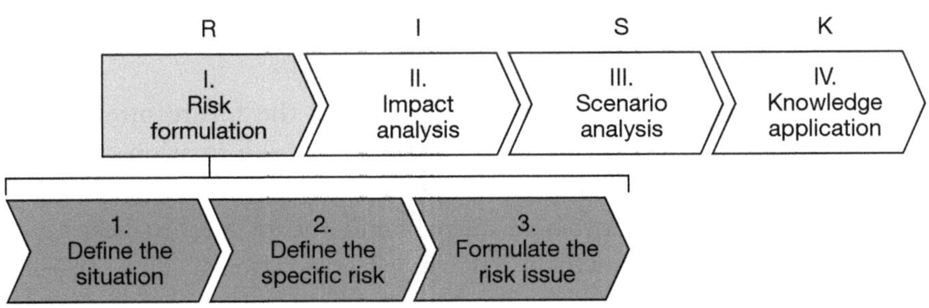

This is the first step of the RISK Rules.

> In Step I it is crucial to formulate the right question because the later steps will provide an answer to this question. Remember that a perfect answer to an inaccurate question will lead to an unwanted strategy. My recommendation is that you spend sufficient effort in defining the risk issue.

Step I consists of three sub-steps:

1. Define the situation.
2. Define the specific risk.
3. Formulate the risk issue.

1. Define the situation

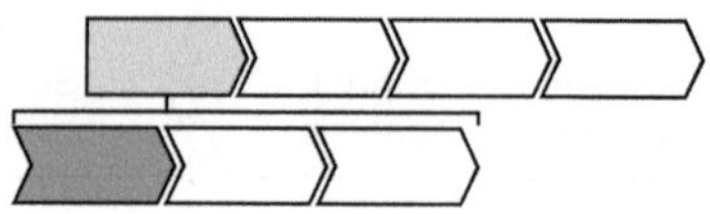

The starting point is to define the situation. The easiest way for you to approach this is by looking into the sources of the firm's exposure to interest rate risk. As we've covered this subject in detail in Chapter 2, I'll only summarise briefly here.

A firm is exposed to interest rate risk under two conditions:

1. It has current or future interest-bearing assets or liabilities.
2. The interest rate is variable now or in the future.

To identify current interest-bearing assets and liabilities, look for the following four balance sheet items:

- Long-term loans
- Short-term loans
- Cash and cash equivalents
- Financial non-current assets

If you work for a firm you will know the future interest-bearing assets and liabilities. Otherwise relevant information can be found in the notes appended to the financial statements.

Make a list of those current and future interest-bearing assets and liabilities which have a variable interest rate. Include all relevant requirements by the firm (from the financial statements) that can be influenced by interest rate movements.

Examples of interest-bearing assets and liabilities

- The firm has a €10 million bullet term loan based on 3-months Euribor with a remaining term of five years.
- Within half a year the firm expects to sign a 7-year $5 million working capital facility based on 1-month USD LIBOR.
- The firm has core cash reserves of £1 million that receive modest credit interest.

Examples of relevant requirements by the firm

- There are financial covenants in the financing arrangements that the firm does not want to breach.
- The firm prefers a stable cash flow.
- The business owner focuses on the highest possible net profit.

The situation: Trader

Define

On the basis of the new financing arrangement, Trader has three sources of interest rate risk:

- Real estate loan
- Current account overdraft
- GBP term loan

The interest payable on the three sources of interest rate risk is based on the following three reference rates in the money market:

- 1-month Euribor
- 3-months Euribor
- 6-months GBP LIBOR

As a result of the three sources of interest rate risk, movements of the three reference rates affect the financial statements of Trader as follows:

- Income statement: the interest line item is directly influenced by changes in the reference rates. The effect trickles down into the earnings before tax and finally into the net profit.
- Cash flow statement: the interest line item is directly influenced by changes in the reference rates.
- Balance sheet: the cash position is directly influenced by changes in the reference rates. As a result net debt (interest-bearing liabilities minus cash) is influenced. Consequently, the net debt / EBITDA ratio is affected. The balance sheet is indirectly

influenced as the effects of reference rate changes on net profit are passed on to the retained earnings when the net profit is not (fully) distributed to the shareholders. In turn, the retained earnings are part of the solvency ratio.

The financing arrangement of Trader includes two financial covenants. (See Chapter 5 for a detailed explanation of financial covenants.) In short, a bank wants to ascertain that a lender can meet its interest and debt redemption obligations. After a bank has transferred the money to its customer, however, it loses control. Through including financial covenants in the financing arrangement, it has an early warning system to detect a possible financial distress situation before it is too late.

Trader's two financial covenants are:

- ICR ratio (EBIT / Interest): the higher the ratio the better, since it is then less likely that Trader will fail to meet its interest payment obligations to the bank.
- Solvency ratio (equity / balance sheet total): an indication of the degree to which Trader can meet its interest and debt redemption obligations to the bank in the event of liquidation.

The management of Trader wants to meet both financial covenants at all times.

2. Define the specific risk

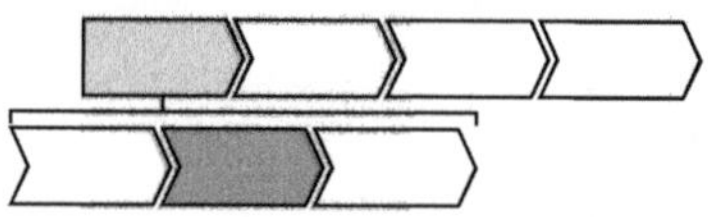

The next stage is to define the specific risk to the firm. Answer the question: if market interest rates fluctuate (strongly), what is the risk to the firm? Where does it go wrong?

Examples of specific risks

- A firm has variable interest-bearing liabilities and if market interest rates increase significantly, it will be struggling to meet interest payable.
- A firm owner wants to be certain to have the cash available for future investments and wants to rule out higher interest rates upsetting his plans.
- A firm has financial covenants in its financing arrangement that it does not want to breach.

The specific risk: Trader

Define

If one of the financial covenants is breached by Trader, the bank can cancel the loans and demand direct repayment. In practice banks usually give some leeway before demanding back all loans. Nevertheless, the bank is entitled to charge penalty payments by increasing the markup on all loans. Furthermore, all legal and other costs that may arise in the resolution of the situation will have to be paid by Trader. That is why Trader wants to take all possible preventive measures to avoid a breach of its financial covenants.

The specific risk for Trader therefore is that:

- The ICR ratio is less than 3.
- The solvency ratio is lower than 25%.

3. Formulate the risk issue

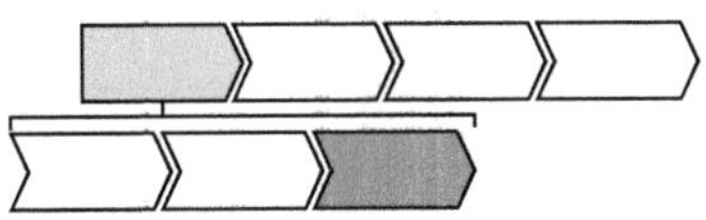

The aim of Step I is to formulate the correct risk issue. You can do this by rephrasing the specific risk you have defined as a question.

Examples of risk questions

- How can the firm hedge interest rate risk so that the interest payable on its long-term loan is maximally 6%?
- How can the firm hedge interest rate risk so that stable future interest payments on its loans are secured?
- How can the firm hedge interest rate risk in order to ensure that the financial covenants in its financing arrangement are not breached?

The risk issue: Trader

Formulate

The management of Trader wants to comply with both financial covenants at all times in order to avoid a possible situation of financial distress. As interest rate volatility is outside the control of management, yet can have a serious negative impact on both financial covenants, management wishes to formulate the best possible interest rate risk management strategy so that it can always meet both financial covenants.

Hence, the risk issue for Trader is defined as follows:

How can Trader formulate an optimal interest rate risk strategy in order to ensure that the ICR ratio of minimally 3 and the solvency ratio of minimally 25% in the financing arrangement are met at all times?

THE MACRAE RISK REDUCTION RULES®

Step II. Impact analysis

Figure 10.3

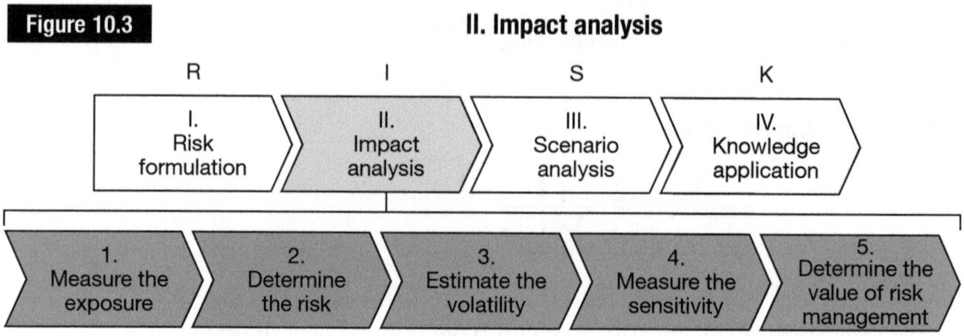

This is the second step of the RISK Rules.

The goal of Step II is to determine if hedging interest rate risk creates value for the firm. This is important because hedging in itself, for instance by using derivatives, does not necessarily create value. On the contrary – as setting up and monitoring a hedging programme costs money and banks charge a margin when a firm buys derivatives, hedging may decrease value. There are some necessary conditions for hedging to make sense and I'll discuss these.

Step II consists of five sub-steps:

1. Measure the exposure.
2. Quantify the risk.
3. Estimate the volatility.
4. Measure the sensitivity.
5. Determine the value of risk management.

1. Measure the exposure

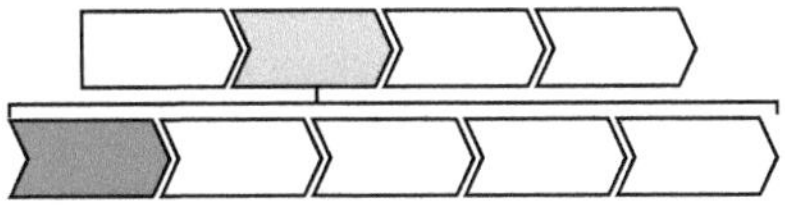

The first sub-step is to list all current and future interest-bearing positions with a variable interest rate. You can use the information from Step I as a basis to work this out. Write down the following details of each interest-bearing asset and liability:

- Source of exposure
- Principal (including debt repayment)
- Term

Examples of exposure measurement

- The firm is exposed to interest rate risk through a variable rate medium-term loan from 15/02/2015 to 15/02/2020 over a principal of £10 million, with annual debt repayment of £2 million.
- The firm is exposed to interest rate risk through a working capital facility with a limit of $5 million which is daily cancellable.
- The firm is exposed to interest rate risk through a 7-year bullet term loan to another firm with a principal of €20 million which has a remaining life of 3 years.

Now check the relevance of your list. Its relevancy depends on the remaining life of the source of exposure and the principal amount. For example, if the principal of a working capital facility is extremely low compared to the principal of long-term loans, you may leave it out of the analysis. Or, if a total refinancing will take place very soon, it is better to focus on the future than on the current sources of exposure. Furthermore, if a loan is nearly repaid, you may decide not to include it in your further analysis.

Measure

The exposure: Trader

First we need to list the current sources of interest rate exposure of Trader. In order to do so, we check the balance sheet presented in Appendix I for the following four sources of interest rate exposure:

- Long-term loans
- Short-term loans
- Cash and cash equivalents
- Financial non-current assets

We use the latest available balance sheet data, which is from 2013.

On the liability side of the balance sheet Trader is exposed to interest rate risk at three sources:

- €35,409,000 secured bank loans – long-term portion
- €2,631,000 current portion of long-term debt
- €22,668,000 short-term financing

On the asset side of the balance sheet Trader is exposed to interest rate risk at two sources:

- €1,935,000 cash and bank
- €1,242,000 financial assets of which €999,000 relates to subsidiaries

From 1 January 2015 Trader has a new financing arrangement fully replacing the old one. The financing arrangement concerns all interest-bearing liabilities. This means that there is no point in using the balance sheet data above with respect to the long-term and short-term loans because they have been fully replaced. For all interest-bearing liabilities we will therefore use the sources of exposure from the new financing arrangement.

With respect to cash and cash equivalents and financial non-current assets we can still use the balance sheet data as the new financing arrangement does not directly influence interest-bearing assets. However, the new financing arrangement does stipulate that Trader receives the bank's variable rate on current account credit balances over €100,000.

From 1 January 2015 Trader's five sources of exposure to interest rate risk with respect to principal (including debt repayment) and term are:

Real estate loan

Principal:	€21,000,000
Principal repayment:	40 instalments of €262,500 and a final instalment of €10,500,000
Term:	10 years, 1 January 2015–31 December 2025

Current account overdraft

Principal:	€48,000,000 credit limit
Principal repayment:	Only when cancelled
Term:	Daily cancellable, starting from 1 January 2015

GBP term loan

Principal:	£4,000,000
Principal repayment:	10 annual instalments of £400,000
Term:	10 years, 1 January 2015–31 December 2025

Cash balances

Principal:	Depending on cash surplus
Principal repayment:	Not applicable
Term:	On a daily basis, starting from 1 January 2015

Financial non-current assets

Trader has financial assets of €1,242,000 in 2013, of which €999,000 relate to subsidiaries. The difference of €243,000 could relate to loans to third parties. However, since this difference in 2012 was only €15,000 (€975,000 – €960,000), it is not likely that there are loans to third parties. Therefore it is assumed that Trader does not have any interest rate exposure in its financial non-current assets. As a result we will exclude the analysis of financial non-current assets from here on.

In conclusion, Trader is exposed to interest rate risk through:

- A real estate loan from 1/1/2015 to 31/12/2025 with a principal of €21,000,000 decreasing by 40 quarterly repayments of €262,500 and a final repayment of €10.5 million.
- Depending on the drawdowns under the current account overdraft up to a maximum of €48 million from 1/1/2015 until cancelled.
- A GBP term loan of £5 million from 1/1/2015 until 31/12/2025 decreasing by £400,000 annually.
- Cash surplus in its current account above €100,000.

2. Determine the risk

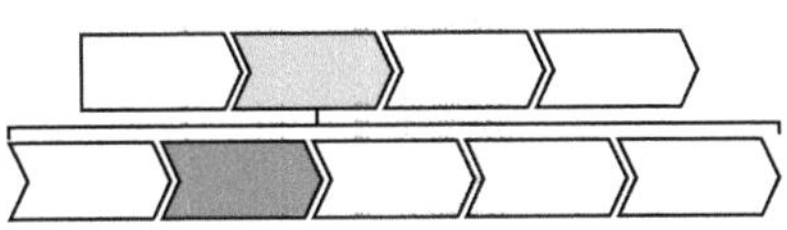

Whereas the first sub-step targets measuring the exposure to interest rate risk, this second sub-step focuses on the clear identification of the interest rate to which the firm is exposed. A separate calculation must be made for each different interest rate. For example, the firm may be exposed to 3-months Euribor, 6-months Euribor, 6-months USD LIBOR and 6-months GBP LIBOR. They are all different interest rates and must therefore be considered separately! However, if a firm has several sources of exposure to the same interest rate, the exposure principals may be added.

The starting point is that the firm is a corporate wishing to manage its interest rate risk. A corporate is primarily concerned with the effects of interest rate movements in its income statement and cash flow statement and is less concerned about the effects on the value of balance sheet items.

Interest rate risk is defined here as an interest rate development that is negative from the firm's point of view. Therefore, a higher than expected interest rate is only a disadvantage in the case of interest-bearing liabilities. The chance of lower interest rates is a risk for firms with interest-bearing assets.

For defining interest rate risk three elements are important:

- The relevant reference rate
- The period of exposure to interest rate risk
- Which development in interest rates would be negative from the firm's point of view

Examples of determining interest rate risk

- The risk is that 3-months Euribor increases during a period of 10 years from the moment of signing of the credit facilities.
- The risk is that 3-months USD LIBOR over the period 15/02/2015 to 15/02/2020 will be higher than the market currently expects.
- The risk is that 1-month GBP LIBOR decreases in the coming 5 years.

Determine

The risk: Trader

Based on its interest-bearing assets and liabilities, Trader is exposed to at least three different interest rates:

- 1-month Euribor
- 3-months Euribor
- 6-months GBP LIBOR
- The bank's variable rate if the current account surplus exceeds €100,000

From the perspective of Trader the risk with respect to its interest-bearing liabilities is that the reference interest rate increases. In contrast, regarding a cash surplus in current account, the risk is that the bank's variable rate decreases.

Per source of exposure to interest rate risk, the risk for Trader therefore is:

Real estate loan

- The risk is that 3-months Euribor will increase over a period of 10 years starting on 1 January 2015.

Current account facility

- The risk is that 1-month Euribor will increase from 1 January 2015 until cancellation of the facility.

GBP term loan

- The risk is that 6-months GBP LIBOR will increase over a period of 10 years starting on 1 January 2015.

Cash balances

- The risk is that the bank's variable rate will decrease from 1 January 2015 until cancellation of the facility.

3. Estimate the volatility

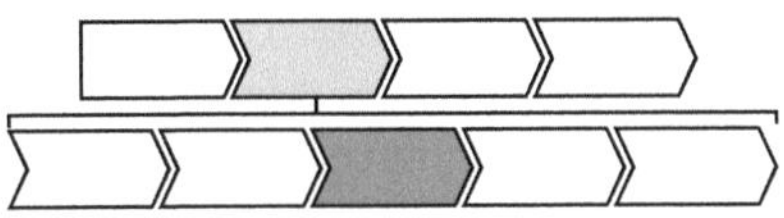

The objective of this stage is to estimate the expected volatility of the reference rate to which the firm is exposed for the exposure horizon. For each interest rate to which the company is exposed you establish a range of probability within which the interest rate in question is expected to fluctuate.

Examples of volatility estimations

- 3-months Euribor is currently 1%, and within the exposure horizon of 15/02/2015 to 15/02/2020, its expected minimum is 0.5% and its expected maximum is 3%.
- The 3-months reference rate is currently 1%. For the coming 10 years a range of 1%–5% is expected.

Since we define interest rate risk as a negative movement in interest rates from the firm's point of view, you could in principle focus on the downside risk only. However, with respect to alternatives to hedging in later steps it is advised to use a range, which includes the upside potential.

Estimate

The volatility: Trader

Trader is exposed to movements in the following reference rates:

- 1-month Euribor
- 3-months Euribor
- 6-months GBP Libor
- The bank's variable rate

For all further calculations, all above mentioned reference rates are currently 1% and the expected range over a period of 10 years is between 1% and 5% for all rates.

4. Measure the sensitivity

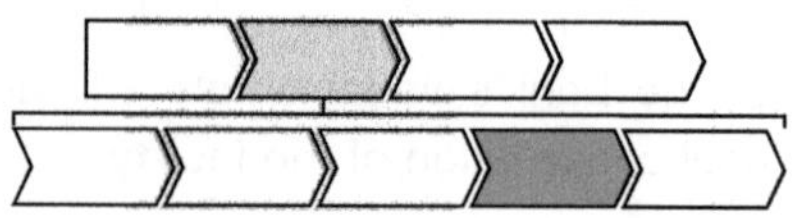

Sensitivity calculates the effect of a change in market interest rates on the interest payable or receivable by the firm. Sensitivity is most easily calculated by measuring the effect of a 1 percentage point movement in the relevant interest rate on interest payable or receivable.

The goal of this sub-step is to calculate the worst-case and best-case scenario for each source of exposure. The worst-case scenario is calculated by multiplying the principal of the interest-bearing position by the worst value in the range of the relevant reference rate you have estimated in the previous sub-step.

If, for example, a firm has a long-term loan with a principal of $10 million and the maximum expected increase in the interest rate is to 6%, the interest payable for this loan would then be estimated at maximally $600,000 yearly. Use this method to calculate the worst-case scenario for each source of exposure. Then add these worst-case totals of interest payable together and you have the maximum interest payable for the firm on the basis of your assumptions with regard to expected volatility. Now make the same calculation per source of exposure using the best-case scenario. You then have the expected range of total interest payable for the firm on the basis of your assumptions with regard to expected volatility of the various interest rates concerned.

Measure

The sensitivity: Trader

Calculations are based on the average principals in the first year after the start of the new financing arrangement on 1 January 2015. The reference rates of all loans are 1%. As Trader intends to minimise current account credit balances in order to minimise inefficiency, this is ignored in the further analysis.

Effect of an increase in 3-months Euribor

The average principal of the real estate loan in 2015 is €20,475,000: the principal of €21,000,000 on 1 January 2015 less repayment of two instalments (2 x €262,500 = €525,000). A 1 percentage point increase of 3-months Euribor will increase the interest payable by Trader by €204,750 (€20,475,000 x 1% = €204,750). The effects of an increase in 3-months Euribor on Trader's interest payable within the range of expected volatility are:

1 percentage point:	*+ €204,750*
2 percentage points:	*+ €409,500*
3 percentage points:	*+ €614,250*
4 percentage points:	*+ €819,000*

Effect of an increase in 1-month Euribor

It is assumed that Trader draws down the maximum amount of its current account overdraft from 1 January 2015 (i.e. €48,000,000). The effect of an increase in 1-month Euribor on Trader's interest payable is:

1 percentage point:	*+ €480,000*
2 percentage points:	*+ €960,000*
3 percentage points:	*+ €1,440,000*
4 percentage points:	*+ €1,920,000*

Effect of an increase in 6-months GBP Libor

The principal in 2015 is £4,000,000 on 1 January 2015 and a repayment of £400,000 will take place at the end of the year. The average principal will therefore be £3,800,000 (£4,000,000 – £200,000). The effect of an increase in 6-months LIBOR on Trader's interest payable is:

1 percentage point: *+ £38,000*

2 percentage points: *+ £76,000*

3 percentage points: *+ £114,000*

4 percentage points: *+ £152,000*

Sensitivity calculations total financing (ceteris paribus)

Table 10.2

Loan	Principal	Reference rate	Markup	Interest payable
Real estate loan	€20,475,000	1.00%	0.90%	€389,025
Current acc. overdraft	€48,000,000	1.00%	1.10%	€1,008,000
GBP term loan	€4,750,000*	1.00%	1.10%	€99,750
Total	**€73,225,000**			**€1,496,775**

*Based on a EUR/GBP rate of 0.80: £3,800,000 × 0.80 = €4,750,000

The starting point is a sensitivity of 0%, or the current reference interest rate of 1%. A 1 percentage point increase in the various reference rates increases Trader's interest payable (in 2015) by €732,250 (total principal of €73,225,000 × 1%).

Table 10.3 shows Trader's sensitivity to future changes in interest rates. The impact of 1, 2, 3 and 4 percentage point increases in the relevant reference rate are displayed.

Table 10.3

Sensitivity (% point)	Reference rate	Interest payable
0%	1.00%	€1,496,775
1%	2.00%	€2,229,025
2%	3.00%	€2,961,275
3%	4.00%	€3,693,525
4%	5.00%	€4,425,775

5. Determine the value of risk management

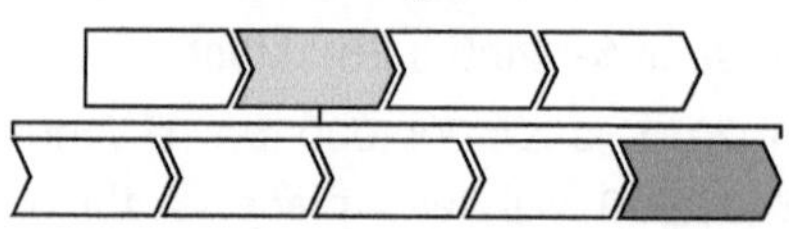

A first necessary condition for risk management creating value for the firm is that the firm is exposed to interest rate risk. Remember the four sources of exposure to interest rate risk. The second necessary condition is that the impact on the financial statements is substantial, otherwise risk management will cost more than it yields. Mitigating interest rate risk does create value, but indirectly. The theory behind creating firm value by hedging interest rate risk is extensively described in Chapter 6. The following four arguments for hedging to create firm value were discussed:

1. Reducing expected taxes
2. Minimising financial distress costs
3. Reducing agency costs
4. Controlling managerialism

Determine

The value of risk management: Trader

The financial distress argument for creating firm value by hedging interest rate risk is especially important for Trader.

The sensitivity of the financial covenants of Trader are calculated:

- ICR
- Solvency

ICR Trader

According to the financing arrangement, the Interest Coverage Ratio (ICR: EBIT / Interest) must minimally be 3. On the basis of the latest available EBIT, namely €9,087,000 in 2014, the calculation is as follows:

€9,087,000 / interest = 3, or interest = €3,029,000

If interest payable exceeds €3,029,000 Trader will breach the limit of 3. What interest rate increase corresponds with that level of interest payable? We calculate with a simultaneous increase of all three reference rates: €3,029,000 – €1,496,775 = €1,532,225; €1,532,225 / €732,250 = 2.10% (rounded). Thus, if interest rates increase by 2.10 percentage points (interest income is ignored), Trader would breach the ICR ratio. This is a clear reason for Trader to hedge interest rate risk from the perspective of financial distress.

Solvency Trader

Trader has a solvency ratio (equity / balance sheet total) of 25% in its new financing arrangement. For every 1 percentage point rise in interest rates, Trader's interest expense increases by €732,250 and its profit before tax falls by the same amount. After tax, assuming a 25% tax rate, the negative effect on net profit is €549,375 per percentage point rise in interest rates. The solvency ratio can be calculated on the basis of the latest available balance sheet figures, which are from 2013: €36,666,000 / €136,416,000 = 26.9%. We want to know at which level of a simultaneous increase of the reference rates the solvency ratio would be breached. This can be found out by solving the following equation: (€36,666,000 – x) / €136,416,000 = 25%; x = €2,562,000; €2,562,000 / €549,375 = 4.66%. In other words, if the reference rates increase by 4.66%, the solvency ratio is breached. The reference rate would then be 5.66% (4.66% + 1% current rate), which is outside the range of expected volatility of 1% to 5%. Nevertheless, any minor negative factor in the operating result could mean that the 25% limit would be breached, in which case the bank would be entitled to call in the facility immediately. An additional factor that would come into play is that often banks will require that if the solvency ratio falls below the agreed level, the firm may not distribute any dividend. This would not be appreciated by Trader's owners.

The graph in Chapter 4 illustrating the development of 3-months Euribor between 1999 and 2014 shows how strong money market rates can fluctuate. For instance, at the end of 2008 this important reference rate decreased by 3.5 percentage points in only six months' time! Of course these are figures from the past. Nevertheless, they illustrate that a 2.10 percentage point or even a 4.66 percentage point increase is (very) plausible.

Conclusions financial distress Trader

The financial distress argument for hedging interest rate risk is a cogent one in Trader's case because Trader is close to breaching its ICR ratio and its solvency ratio is not fully safe either.

THE MACRAE RISK REDUCTION RULES®

Step III. Scenario analysis

Figure 10.4

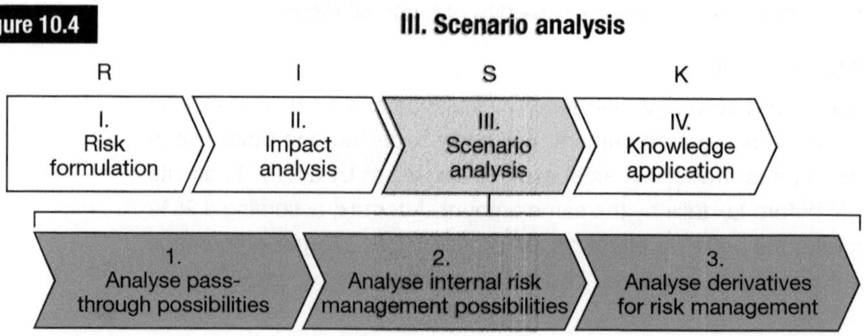

This is the third step of the RISK Rules.

> The goal of Step III is to examine how the interest rate risk of a firm can be hedged and whether there are other, more structural ways of mitigating risk than by using derivatives.

Step III consists of three sub-steps:

1. Analyse pass-through possibilities
2. Analyse internal risk management possibilities
3. Analyse derivatives for risk management

1. Analyse pass-through possibilities

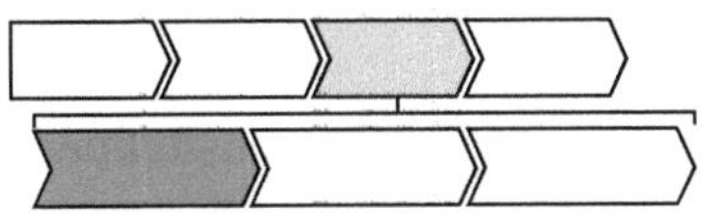

If the previous sub-step (the value of risk management) shows that the firm can benefit from reducing its interest rate risk, the next step is to see whether it is able to pass interest rate risk on to third parties (pass-through), such as to its customers and suppliers. Pass-through implies that if interest rates rise, the firm can pass the higher interest on to its customers. Since inflation is an important component in the interest rate, this is often referred to as an inflation adjustment. The advantage of pass-through compared to using derivatives is that the former solution is a more structural way of reducing risk than the latter.

Pass-through can be accomplished in two ways:

- Pricing
- Contractually

Pricing

Whether it is possible to pass negative interest rate developments to customers by means of higher prices depends very much on the structure of the market in which the firm operates. If the firm has a monopoly or the market is an oligopoly (a small number of providers with large market shares), it is possible that the firm will be able to pass negative interest rate movements on. In a market with many customers and many providers, the opportunity for pass-through is extremely low. In this case firms sell on the basis of price. Firms will price themselves out of the market if they raise their prices when inflation rises: customers will simply go to another supplier.

Contractually

The firm can make contractual agreements with its suppliers and customers regarding the level of prices in relation to inflation. This mainly applies to long-term (framework) contracts. Contracts may include limits or bandwidths for inflation and agreements with regard to the adjustment of prices.

Analyse

Pass-through possibilities: Trader

Trader is not in a position to pass through interest rate risk to third parties.

2. Analyse internal risk management possibilities

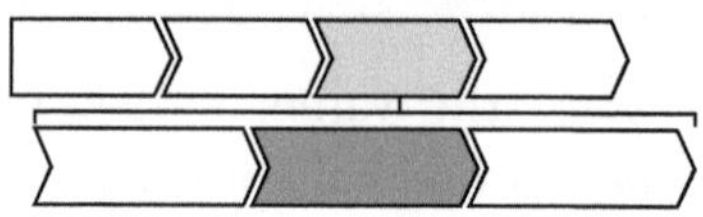

Like pass-through, internal hedging is a more permanent way of reducing interest rate risk than using derivatives. A firm can hedge internally by matching its interest-bearing assets with interest-bearing liabilities. In that case the exposure remains unchanged, but interest rate risk is reduced. The basic principle is that a similar reference rate applies to the assets and to the liabilities, and that the maturities overlap.

Example

Internal risk management possibilities

A firm has an overdraft facility on the basis of 1-month USD LIBOR. At the same time it has cash available that it will not use for a certain period. The firm receives no interest on positive cash balances. The firm therefore is exposed to the risk that 1-month USD LIBOR increases.

Assets	Liabilities
Intangible non-current assets	Equity:
Property, plant and equipment	Share capital
Financial non-current assets	Reserves
Total non-current assets	**Total equity**
Inventory	Provisions
Receivables	Long-term loans
Cash and cash equivalents	Short-term loans
Total current assets	**Total current liabilities**

No credit interest (Cash and cash equivalents)

1-month USD LIBOR (Short-term loans)

By matching the reference rate of interest-bearing assets and liabilities, while the exposures still exist, interest rate risk is (temporarily) decreased for the amount of the lower of the two principals.

Inventory	Provisions
Receivables	Long-term loans
Cash and cash equivalents	Short-term loans
Total current assets	**Total current liabilities**

1-month USD LIBOR (Cash and cash equivalents)

1-month USD LIBOR (Short-term loans)

The question is, however, how long this type of internal reduction of interest rate risk can continue in view of the normal mismatch in term. Current account overdrafts and medium- and long-term loans in general are taken out for a longer period while cash balances are usually held only in the shorter term. The situation is different for interest-bearing loans to third parties, which are generally provided for a longer period.

If a firm uses its surplus cash to repay debt, both the exposure and the interest rate risk are reduced.

Go through your list of sources of exposure to interest rate risk to see whether the firm is able to hedge internally by matching its interest-bearing assets and liabilities. If so, remove the interest rate exposure in question from the list.

Analyse

Internal risk management possibilities: Trader

As it is Trader's intention to minimise its cash surplus by efficient cash management, internal hedging possibilities are not likely. However, in a case where an excess cash position exists for a longer period of time, Trader can match the interest rate on its cash position with the funds drawn down under its current account overdraft on the basis of 1-month Euribor.

3. Analyse derivatives for risk management

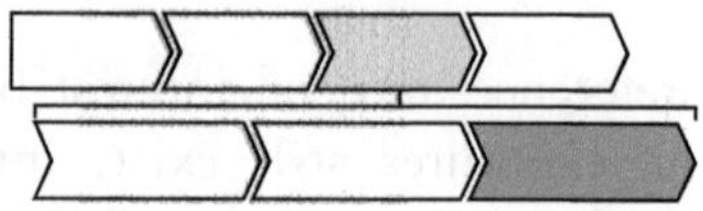

The remainder of a firm's exposure to interest rate risk that can neither be passed through to third parties nor hedged internally can be hedged with derivatives. Two factors should be considered:

- The hedging horizon
- The hedging percentage

Hedging horizon

Hedging horizon means the term of the derivative compared to the term of the underlying exposure. Basically, fixing the interest for 3 months is as much of a hedge as fixing the interest for 5 years. If a firm purchases short-term derivatives, however, these will actually to a large extent move with the yield curve. In other words, the reduction in risk will have (very) limited effect. The longer the term of the derivative, the more effective the hedge becomes because the amount of interest payable or receivable in future becomes more certain. In principle the following is recommended: the greater a firm's sensitivity to interest rate movements, the longer the hedging horizon should be.

Hedging percentage

The hedging percentage means the portion of the firm's exposure that is hedged: the principal of the hedge compared to the principal of the exposure. The higher the hedging percentage, the more certain the firm can be with regard to the interest payable or receivable in the future. The hedging percentage depends on the firm's sensitivity to interest rate movements. The greater the sensitivity of the firm to interest rate fluctuations, the higher the hedging percentage should be.

When choosing the appropriate hedging horizon and hedging percentage, be aware of the issues that can arise due to overhedging with derivatives, which are analysed in Part 1.

There are two important factors with regard to the hedging percentage:

- Sensitivity to interest rate movements
- A view with respect to interest rate developments

Sensitivity to interest rate movements

The firm's sensitivity to interest rate movements should be the primary driver for hedging. For instance, if a firm is close to the limits set in its financial covenants, choosing the highest possible hedging percentage is of primary importance.

A view with respect to interest rate developments

A view with regard to interest rates is of secondary importance, and can only be taken into account at a time when the firm can allow itself to do so – in other words, if the firm can absorb the negative effects of interest rate movements.

When considering incorporating a personal view when hedging interest rate risk, see the issues in Part 1 on deliberate speculation with derivatives.

In conclusion, the sensitivity of a firm to interest rate movements is the leading consideration for the hedging horizon, the hedging percentage, and for the consideration of an interest rate view. The greater the effect of interest rate movements, the longer the hedging horizon, the higher the hedging percentage and the less significant the view on interest rates becomes.

Choice of linear derivatives or options

When considering the type of derivative to use, you have to take into account the certainty of the underlying exposure. For instance, under normal conditions current interest rate exposures are more certain than future interest rate exposures. The basic approach is that exposures that are uncertain should be hedged with options and exposures that are certain can be hedged with either linear derivatives or options. For extensive information of derivatives, see Chapter 8 on linear derivatives and Chapter 9 on options.

Hence, the first choice is whether to use linear derivatives or optional instruments. The second choice is to make a selection from the possible derivatives available. This depends on the firm's reasons for hedging. The less financial room the firm has and the more urgent its need to hedge, the more likely it is that it should select plain vanilla derivatives. The more financial room the firm has, the more possibility there is for more complicated derivatives.

At this stage it is key to identify all possible derivatives to hedge the interest rate risk, so don't limit the number of possible solutions.

Analyse

Derivatives for risk management: Trader

Regarding the ICR as a financial covenant, we have earlier calculated that if the reference rates increase by 2.10 percentage points the ICR ratio is breached. This requires a strict risk management policy. With respect to the solvency ratio, a rise of the interest rates by 4.66 percentage points to 5.66% would lead to a breach of the covenant. Although this level of the reference rates would be outside the expected volatility of maximally 5%, a breach of the solvency ratio covenant is not totally unthinkable.

Since a breach of one of its financial covenants would mean that Trader's loans could be called in by the bank immediately, the wisest course for Trader is to avoid this situation and to hedge its interest rate risk. Given the imminent danger of breaching the ICR ratio it is not recommended for Trader to include a personal view on interest rate developments, at least not before the ratios have significantly improved.

It is advisable to hedge the real estate loan and the GBP term loan using derivatives for the entire life of 10 years, matched to the repayment schedule. For Trader's current account facilities, the level of drawdown and the term are uncertain (formally these facilities may be cancelled at a day's notice). The term of the hedge should preferably be for as long as Trader's financial planning allows.

THE MACRAE RISK REDUCTION RULES®

Step IV. Knowledge application

Figure 10.5

IV. Knowledge application

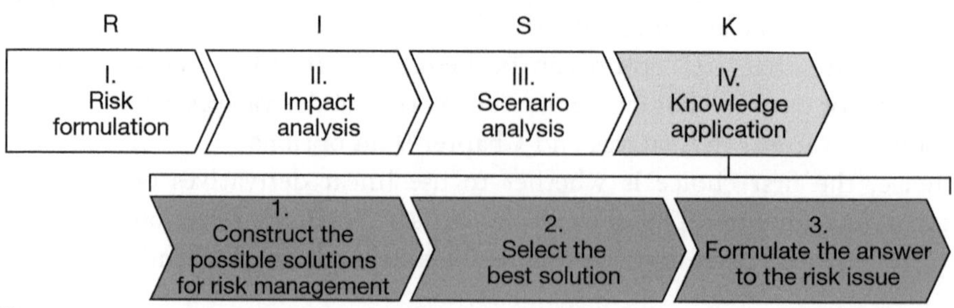

This is the final step of the RISK Rules.

> Key in Step IV is to provide an answer to the risk issue established in Step I.

Step IV of the Rules consists of three sub-steps:

1. Construct the possible solutions for risk management.
2. Select the best solution.
3. Formulate the answer to the risk issue.

1. Construct the possible solutions for risk management

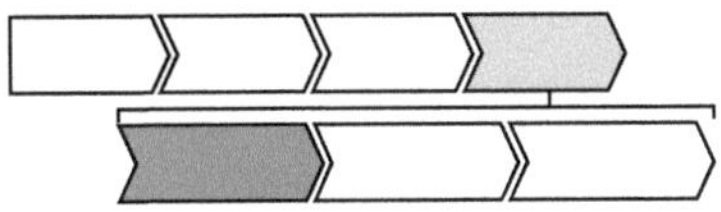

List the possible solutions that can mitigate the risk issue established in Step I: it is a combination of the goals for risk management and all possible solutions to reach those goals. You could use a matrix, as presented below, to support the analysis. All goals for risk management are presented horizontally and all possible solutions to reach the goals are presented vertically. Theoretically, you should do this per source of exposure to interest rate risk. Some solutions will achieve the goals better than others: tick the relevant boxes. Using a matrix will provide you with a clear overview, especially if there are many goals and solutions.

Table 10.4

Matrix

	Avoid breach of financial covenant: ICR	Stable interest cash flow
Internal risk management		
Swaps		
Cap		
Collar		

Construct

The possible solutions for risk management: Trader

The matrix for Trader is similar for the real estate loan and the GBP term loan:

	ICR ratio	Solvency ratio
Swaps	√√√	√√√
Cap	√	√√√
Collar	√√	√√√

For the current account overdraft the matrix is different due to its daily cancellability:

	ICR ratio	Solvency ratio
Swaps	√	√
Cap	√√	√√√
Collar	√√√	√√√

In order to ensure that primarily the ICR ratio and secondarily the solvency ratio are not breached, all exposure to interest rate risk should be hedged as far as possible. The checkmarks in the matrix indicate the attractiveness of different derivatives for hedging. There is less leeway with respect to hedging the ICR ratio than hedging the solvency ratio as the former ratio is closer to being breached.

Trader should hedge the real estate loan and the GBP term loan with derivatives over the full term of 10 years based on the debt redemption schedule. Theoretically, both swaps and options (or a combination) are possible.

For the current account overdraft both the level of drawdown and the term are uncertain. Trader should make the term of the hedge for the working capital facilities as long as the financial planning of the firm reasonably allows. It is advisable to use options instead of linear instruments in order to be able to deal with the aforementioned uncertainties, while at the same time fully hedging interest rate risk. By using options, Trader does not run the risk of overhedging with respect to the term nor with respect to the principal of the derivatives: see the derivatives blunders on overhedging described in Part 1.

2. Select the best solution

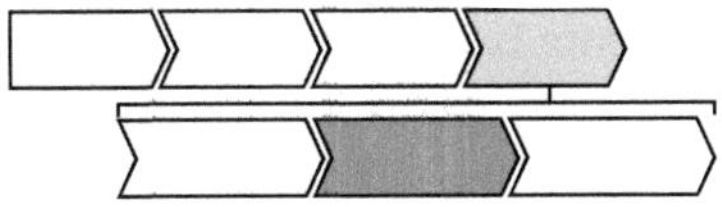

Select the best solution from the list you've made in the previous sub-step and give the arguments for doing so.

The best solution: Trader

Select

As Trader is close to breaching the ICR ratio and options require the firm to pay an option premium, which is represented in the interest line in the income statement and therefore directly impacts the ICR ratio, options are not advised for hedging the real estate loan and the GBP term loan. Conversely, using options is advocated for hedging the core part of the working capital facilities in order to avoid overhedging. In order to minimise interest expenses, Trader is advised to use a zero cost collar to hedge interest risk from the working capital facilities. If there is room for a (small) option premium, a regular collar could be opted for.

3. Formulate the answer to the risk issue

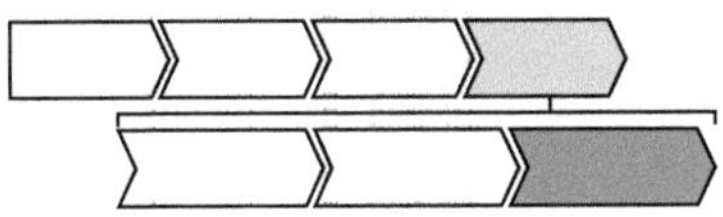

Use the best solution from the previous sub-step to formulate an answer to the risk issue that you determined in Step I.

The answer to the risk issue: Trader

Formulate

In Step I the risk use was defined as follows:

How can Trader formulate an optimal interest rate risk strategy in order to ensure that the ICR ratio of minimally 3 and the solvency ratio of minimally 25% in the financing agreement are met at all times?

In order to ensure that the ICR and the solvency ratios are not breached, the answer to the risk issue is:

1. Real estate loan: fully hedge with interest rate swaps over the entire term of 10 years based on the debt redemption schedule.
2. Current account overdraft: hedge the core exposure with a (zero cost) collar. The term of the hedge should be as long as financial planning allows.

3. GBP term loan: fully hedge with interest rate swaps over the entire term of 10 years based on the debt redemption schedule.
4. Cash and cash equivalents: in the case of a longer-term current account surplus, match the reference rate with that of the current account facility (1-month Euribor).

Afterword

Many methods have been devised for formulating a corporate strategy, and many books have been written on the subject, but I have seen very few comprehensive guides to establishing a corporate interest rate risk strategy.

Starting this book with derivatives blunders was deliberately provocative. It was meant to show that there is an issue that needs to be solved. If in the future there are fewer newspaper headlines on derivatives blunders and the mis-selling of derivatives, then perhaps this book will have contributed to this. In that case it will have achieved its goal of enhancing understanding of a firm's interest rate risk and of the risk arising from derivatives use.

A second reason for beginning the book with derivatives blunders is that a demonstration of how *not* to do something points us in the right direction for finding a solution. The analysis of what can go wrong using interest rate derivatives is strongly intertwined with the rest of the book and provides valuable information on how to use the right techniques.

As with a recipe in a cookbook, formulating a strategy for interest rate risk remains a craft. Having said that, when the ingredients are known the risk of making an error is reduced. As I have seen many financial professionals mastering the RISK Reduction Rules and its underlying line of reasoning, I am confident that you too will have benefited from reading this book, and in turn will contribute to further understanding of the topic.

Appendices

I Central case, Trader

II Proof of the analytical method

III MiFID customer protection regulations regarding derivatives

APPENDIX I

Central case, Trader

This central case is introduced to support Chapters 5 and 10. In Chapter 5 the case exemplifies the impact of interest rate risk on the financial statements of the firm. In Chapter 10 the case illustrates each step of the analytical method so that it comes to life. The name of the firm in the central case is Trader.

Trader is a European trading company that operates in the automotive sector. It has various subsidiaries across Europe and also has a branch in the United Kingdom. The functional currency of Trader is the euro.

Trader's primary revenue source is the wholesale spare parts business. It buys products in large quantity from mass spare parts producers which are located in various countries. It sells to local customers that require fast delivery of a specific range of products. Trader is known by its customers for having most products in stock and for its prompt delivery.

As a result of its business operations and the financial policy of the management, Trader is exposed to interest rate risk through four possible sources of exposure:

- Long-term loans
- Short-term loans
- Cash and cash equivalents
- Financial non-current assets

It has two financial covenants in its financing arrangement:

- ICR > 3
- Solvency > 25%

The financial statements of Trader are presented below:

- Balance sheet
- Income statement
- Cash flow statement

Balance sheet Trader

Figures x €1,000 at 31 December	2011	2012	2013
ASSETS			
Net intangible assets	1,767	1,161	615
Net property, plant and equipment	14,214	24,762	29,199
Financial assets	1,158	1,005	1,242
Of which subsidiaries	960	975	999
TOTAL FIXED ASSETS	**17,139**	**26,928**	**31,056**
Inventory (excl. work in process)	49,143	53,406	60,696
Accounts receivable trade	32,607	32,646	39,579
Of which intercompany accounts	1,548	825	444
Other current assets	3,249	2,535	3,150
Cash and bank	2,226	2,673	1,935
TOTAL CURRENT ASSETS	**87,225**	**91,260**	**105,360**
TOTAL ASSETS	**104,364**	**118,188**	**136,416**
LIABILITIES			
Share capital	10,209	10,209	10,209
Cumulative retained earnings	23,658	25,104	26,457
TOTAL NET WORTH	**33,867**	**35,313**	**36,666**
Minority interest	81	159	210
RISK-BEARING CAPITAL	**33,948**	**35,472**	**36,876**
Retirements	489	432	486
Deferred taxes	1,779	2,280	2,559
Other operational provisions	150	144	969
TOTAL PROVISIONS	**2,418**	**2,856**	**4,014**
Secured bank loans – long-term portion	12,810	37,956	35,409
TOTAL LONG-TERM LIABILITIES	**12,810**	**37,956**	**35,409**
Current portion long-term debt	2,235	2,667	2,631
Short-term financing	30,306	9,885	22,668
Accounts payable trade	13,281	20,646	25,158
Of which intercompany < 1 year		423	33
Other current liabilities	9,366	8,706	9,660
TOTAL CURRENT LIABILITIES	**55,188**	**41,904**	**60,117**
TOTAL LIABILITIES	**104,364**	**118,188**	**136,416**

Income statement Trader

Figures x €1,000	2011	2012	2013	2014*
Net sales	**221,352**	**235,752**	**266,613**	**281,571**
3rd party	164,994	178,881	204,894	213,003
Gross income	**56,358**	**56,871**	**61,719**	**68,568**
Other income				-1,830
Total income	56,358	56,871	61,719	66,738
Labour costs	26,592	27,948	27,744	30,258
Other expenses	19,569	21,033	23,091	24,414
Sustainable EBITDA	**10,197**	**7,890**	**10,884**	**12,066**
Non-recurring expenses	-1,434	-939	-51	
EBITDA	**11,631**	**8,829**	**10,935**	**12,066**
Depreciation/Amortisation	1,857	1,896	2,331	2,979
EBIT	**9,774**	**6,933**	**8,604**	**9,087**
Interest paid	2,103	2,646	3,396	3,561
Income from subsidiaries	-30	96	72	
EBT	**7,641**	**4,383**	**5,280**	**5,526**
Income taxes	2,763	1,539	1,917	1,980
Net income before extraordinary items	4,878	2,844	3,363	3,546
Minority interest	-15	81	51	
Net income	**4,893**	**2,763**	**3,312**	**3,546**
Reconciliation retained earnings		-1,317	-1,959	-30,003

*Projection

Cash flow statement Trader

Figures x €1,000	2012	2013	2014*
Net income	2,763	3,312	3,546
Total depreciation, amortisation and impairments	1,896	2,331	2,979
Interest paid	2,646	3,396	3,561
Other non-operating items	-96	-72	
Other non-cash items	-939	-51	30
Gross operating cash flow	**6,270**	**8,916**	**10,116**
Net working capital	3,063	-9,711	75,117
Other changes in current assets/ liabilities	54	339	-6,510
Net cash from operations	**9,387**	**-456**	**78,723**
Interest paid	-2,646	-3,396	-3,561
Current portion long-term debt	-2,235	-2,667	-2,661
Financing payments	**-4,881**	**-6,063**	**-6,222**
Net cash income	**4,506**	**-6,519**	**72,501**
Net investment in intangibles	-72	-24	615
Net investment in fixed assets	-10,827	-6,147	26,220
Net investment in financial assets	153	-237	1,242
Cash flow from investments	**10,746**	**-6,408**	**28,077**
Cash surplus/ deficit	**-6,240**	**-12,927**	**100,578**
Shares issued cash			-10,209
Minority interest	78	51	-210
Changes in long-term finance	27,813	84	-35,409
Changes in short-term finance	20,421	12,783	-22,668
Cash flow from financing	**7,470**	**12,918**	**-68,496**
Changes in provisions	438	1,158	-4,014
Other non-operating items (add back)	96	72	
Unreconciled retained earnings	-1,317	-1,959	-30,003
Changes in cash and banks	**447**	**-738**	**-1,935**

*Projection

APPENDIX II

Proof of the analytical method

The analytical method has been tried and tested in the following ways:

1. The analytical method has been licensed to the treasury sales department of a major Dutch bank and was distributed internationally in a training manual. It was thoroughly checked by the staff of the treasury sales department before distribution. All treasury sales advisors must read the manual and are tested on their knowledge of the analytical method and its use in practice. Furthermore, dozens of treasury sales advisors of the bank are working with the analytical method on a daily basis. In assessments I have examined the treasury advisors on their knowledge and correct use of the analytical method.
2. The analytical method has been used for training purposes for treasury sales advisors of large (international) banks, such as Rabobank, ING Bank and Deutsche Bank (Frankfurt).
3. The analytical method has been used for guest lectures at universities, such as Rotterdam School of Management, De Vlerick management school and Nyenrode business university.
4. Summaries of the analytical method have been published in magazines.
5. The analytical method was presented at a meeting of the DACT (Dutch Association of Corporate Treasurers).
6. On behalf of corporates wishing to set up a tailor-made interest rate risk strategy for their firm, the analytical method was used to analyse the situation and provide expert advice.
7. The fundamentals of the analytical method are based on scientific papers that were used for my PhD research.
8. I have used the knowledge and experience gained from working in the treasury department of large (listed) firms such as publishing company Wolters Kluwer and dairy cooperative Friesland Campina.

The above list refers to the analytical method 1.0. Meanwhile, it has been upgraded to 2.0 by adding strategy consulting techniques and by upgrading the graphical presentation. The underlying features of the analytical method have remained the same.

APPENDIX III

MiFID customer protection regulations regarding derivatives

INTRODUCTION

In most interest rate risk strategies derivatives play an important part. When banks advise their clients on derivatives or sell derivatives to them, these activities are regulated in order to protect the customer. This is the reason why it is necessary for all financial professionals dealing with interest rate risk to be aware of the guidelines. As a large number of the financial professionals reading this book will be either working in the EU, or may indirectly be affected by EU regulations, we'll spend some time here investigating the most important customer protection regulations under MiFID. MiFID stands for Markets in Financial Instruments Directive and is binding for all member states of the European Union as well as for Norway, Lichtenstein and Iceland.

As a financial professional you should be aware of your rights and obligations under MiFID. To emphasise its importance, the newspaper headlines below show that infringement of these regulations can lead to massive customer claims.

Newspaper headlines

'£22bn threat to banks in latest mis-selling "scandal" that could rival PPI payouts', *The Independent*, 23 June 2014

'... An investigation by *The Independent* of the potential liabilities of British banks incurred from the mis-selling of interest rate protection products, known as swaps, has revealed that payouts could match the PPI scandal, which has so far cost them £22bn. Lloyds' exposure has been estimated for *The Independent* to be a potential £5bn – and other UK banks could be similarly hit. Until now estimates of the scale of the scandal have been limited to interest-rate hedging products (IRHPs) sold mostly to small and medium-sized businesses. But claims from so-called "sophisticated" clients – those with swaps valued above £10m or who employ 50 people or more – could push the total far higher. *The Independent*, in conjunction with derivative analysts in the City who cannot be identified for legal reasons, examined high-value claims excluded from the Financial Conduct Authority's recent review of mis-selling ...'

'UK banks in mis-selling scandal pay out less than half of refund pot', *Reuters*, 14 October 2014

'Britain's biggest banks have paid out less than 40 percent of the 4 billion pounds ($6.4 billion) set aside to cover the mis-selling of complex interest rate hedging products, according to data from the financial regulator ... The Financial Conduct Authority (FCA) last year ordered banks to review 29,500 cases for possible mis-selling after finding "serious failings" in how interest rate swaps were sold to small businesses ...'

'Banks set aside £700m for swaps scandal', *Financial Times*, 31 January 2013

'Barclays, HSBC, Royal Bank of Scotland and Lloyds have set aside about £700m for compensation for mis-selling complex derivative products to small businesses but analysts suggest the final cost to the industry of the latest mis-selling scandal could be up to £2bn. The Financial Services Authority on Thursday ordered the four banks to review all their sales of interest rate hedging products, including swaps and more complicated products, to small businesses that it concluded were "unlikely to understand the risks associated with those products" ... Interest rate derivatives are supposed to protect businesses against rising interest rates. But in a pilot study of 173 interest rate products, the FSA found that nine out of 10 products sold to small and medium-sized businesses by the four banks failed to meet regulatory requirements and that a "significant" portion of customers should receive compensation ...'

I realise that the MiFID material is somewhat dry and that there is a great deal of legal terminology involved. There is no getting around this unfortunately, but I'll try to be as concrete as possible.

MiFID has three overarching principles that apply to banks and investment firms in order to protect their customers:

- To act honestly, fairly and professionally, in accordance with the best interests of the client.
- To provide the client with services that take account of his individual circumstances.

- To provide the client with appropriate and comprehensive information which is fair, clear, and not misleading.

Based on these overarching principles, there are three particularly important areas within MiFID regarding derivatives and customer protection that you as a financial professional in the area of interest rate risk should be fully aware of, not least because legal issues that have arisen as a result of infringements of MiFID seem to focus on these three specific areas. MiFID requires an investment firm:

1. To have clear procedures in place to **categorise** its clients.
2. To assess the client's **suitability** for certain investment products or services.
3. To provide clients with **information** that is fair, clear and not misleading.

After introducing MiFID, I will elaborate on each of these three requirements separately. At the end, I will briefly introduce the enhanced regulations under MiFID II with which banks and investment firms will have to comply in 2017.

INTRODUCING MIFID

Background

In 1999, the European Commission presented the Financial Services Action Plan. This project was set up to perfect the European internal market for financial services and markets in order to improve the global competitive position of Europe and to stimulate the European economy. The European Commission wanted to promote an integrated, efficient and competitive market by streamlining the appropriate regulations and, where necessary, harmonizing them. MiFID was an important step towards this.

MiFID was issued in 2004 by the European Parliament and the European Council and has been in force since November 2007. It governs the provision of investment services in financial instruments by banks and investment firms and the operation of traditional stock exchanges and alternative trading venues. MiFID replaced the ISD, the Investment Services Directive from 1993, which addressed the performance of services in the area of investments securities. ISD had major shortcomings. In practice, it was unable to guarantee that investment firms could perform activities throughout the EU on the grounds of a permit from the member state in which they originated. In addition, ISD contained outdated rules for the protection of customers.

The MiFID Implementation Directive is legally binding and is directly applicable in the national legal systems of the EU member states. MiFID and the execution measures related to it are structured in accordance with the recommendations of Alexandre Lamfalussy in 2001. He recommended that European regulations be formulated first at the framework level, and only then expanded at the detailed level. The reasoning behind this is so that the basic principles at the highest level can be formulated more quickly, and made to conform more closely with the market situation at the lower level. Four levels are distinguished:

- Level 1: the highest level is MiFID itself; it is a framework directive and only contains top-level standards.
- Level 2: these are execution measures and the framework regulations of MiFID (Level 1) are detailed here. The European Commission has developed the standards in greater detail, which has resulted in two execution measures:
  - The MiFID Implementation Directive, which details the most important structuring requirements and rules of conduct;
  - The MiFID Implementation Regulation, which details the most important requirements in the area of transparency and transaction reporting.
- Level 3: this level is primarily concerned with inserting Level 1 and Level 2 into the national legislation and regulations of the European member states, and with cooperation between the various regulators. More important elements in this implementation are the coordination between the various regulators and the efforts to realize a joint approach in further extrapolating the regulations and implementation of the supervision.

  The CESR (Committee of European Securities Regulators) publishes at Level 3, with the intention of providing guidance in a number of important subjects, such as in the area of inducement, transaction reporting and best execution. The purpose of the CESR in this is to guide regulators in dealing with certain regulations.
- Level 4: the lowest level relates to enforcement and monitoring of the implementation procedures. The European Commission monitors whether the member states implement MiFID correctly and on time. If this is not the case, it can take appropriate measures.

Objectives

MiFID was intended to thoroughly revise the existing legislation of the EU member states, and to harmonise national regulations for financial markets. It aims to realise a comprehensive supervisory and regulatory framework for the organised execution of transactions for investors through stock exchanges, other trading systems and investment firms. The intention of MiFID is to improve facilitation of cross-border service provision, to increase integrity and transparency in the EU markets and to promote competition between the traditional stock exchanges and other trading systems. This encourages innovation, reduces transaction costs and makes more funds available for investment, which will ultimately have a stimulating effect on economic growth. In summary, the objectives of MiFID are:

- To realise an efficient and integrated European market for investment services and activities in which the interests of investors are adequately protected.
- To facilitate the cross-border provision of services by investment firms.

Through MiFID a permit from the regulator in its member state of origin gives a bank or an investment firm the right to offer the same services in another member state. Such a permit can thus be used as a 'European passport'. Investment firms which are not established in a member state of the EU must possess a permit from one of the member states if they wish to provide investment services to customers in the EU. Investment firms from Australia, the United States and Switzerland are exempt from the permit obligation inasmuch as their investment services are regulated and they can demonstrate this. These investment firms cannot possess a European passport if they make use of this exemption. A permit will be issued to an investment firm if the investment firm can demonstrate that it meets the permit requirements, which are, briefly:

- Expertise
- Reliability
- Ethical business operations policy
- Minimum number of policymakers and location of performance of work
- Control structure
- Structure of business operations
- Separation of assets
- Policy to prevent conflicts of interests
- Minimum equity
- Requirements for a Multilateral Trading Facility (MTF) – if applicable

MiFID has fully harmonised the code of conduct and the organisational requirements. It takes into account the different character of investment services and activities, the professionalism of investors and the nature of different financial instruments. Moreover, MiFID expands the scope of the European passport. Since MiFID came into effect, the European passport has also covered the issue of investment advice, the operation of a MTF, systematic internalisation and the provision of investment services and performance of investment activities in the context of commodities derivatives.

Scope

You'll find that the term 'investment firm' is often used with respect to MiFID. An investment firm includes banks, but is not limited to banks. In line with MiFID terminology, from now on we'll use the term 'investment firm' and will not mention banks separately.

MiFID defines an investment firm as a party providing an investment service or performing an investment activity. MiFID defines the provision of an investment service as:

- Receiving and passing on customers' orders with regard to financial instruments, in the performance of a profession or business.
- Execution of customers' orders with regard to financial instruments at the expense of customers, in the performance of a profession or business.
- Management of an individual capital.
- Providing advice on financial instruments in the provision of a profession or business.
- The taking over or placement of financial instruments by offering them with a placement guarantee, in the provision of a profession or business.
- Placement of financial instruments by offering them without a placement guarantee, in the provision of a profession or business.

MiFID defines the provision of an investment activity as:

- Trading at one's own expense in the performance of a profession or business.
- Operating a multilateral trading facility in the performance of a profession or business.

MiFID recognises the following financial instruments:

- Share.

- Bond.
- Money market instrument.
- Right to participate in an investment institution, which is not a security.
- An option, future, swap, interest rate or other futures contract or other derivatives contract relating to securities, currency, base interest rates, yields or other derivative instruments, indices or standards, and which can be settled by means of material delivery or in cash.
- An option, future, swap, interest rate or other futures contract or other derivatives contract relating to commodities and which can or must be settled in cash at the choice of one of the parties, unless the reason is a failure to pay or another event which results in termination of the contract.
- An option, future, swap or other derivatives contract relating to commodities which can only be settled by means of material delivery, and which is traded on a regulated market or a multilateral trading facility.
- An option, future, swap or futures contract other than those referred to above or another derivatives contract relating to commodities which can be settled by means of material delivery and is not intended for commercial purposes, and which has the characteristics of other derivative financial instruments.
- Derivative instrument for the transfer of credit risk.
- Financial contract to settle differences.
- An option, future, swap, futures contract or other derivatives contract relating to climate variables, freight fees, emission permits, inflation percentages or other official economic statistics and which must or can, at the request of one of the parties, be settled in cash, other than on the grounds of a failure or other resolutive element or derivatives contract relating to assets, rights, obligations, indices or measures other than those listed above, and which possess the characteristics of other derivative financial instruments.

Customer classification

An important objective of MiFID is to protect investors. It recognises that investors have different levels of knowledge, skills and expertise and as a result it distinguishes three categories of clients. To each category MiFID attaches a different – increasing – regulatory level of protection. The basic principle is that the more professional the customer, the more he is able to independently understand which risks are attached to investment services or transactions.

An investment firm must have clear procedures in place to categorise its clients and to assess their suitability for each type of investment product. The customer classification should be clear to all parties involved from the outset. Not only can the general customer classification be changed by means of a written confirmation between both parties, but it is also possible to have a different customer classification for different services or transactions or for different types of products!

The three categories are:

1. Eligible counterparties
2. Professional clients
3. Retail clients (also called non-professional clients)

I will elaborate on these below, and will then discuss how clients can change from one category to the other.

1. Eligible counterparties

Eligible counterparties are considered to be the most sophisticated investors and have the lowest level of protection. Investment firms are allowed to enter into derivatives transactions with eligible counterparties with only a light touch regulatory regime under MiFID. This means that a large proportion of the rules of conduct are not applicable, such as those relating to information provision, provisions relating to the customer profile, trading in the interest of the investor and best execution. Important to note is that an eligible counterparty does not receive any investment advice. The entities listed below are automatically recognised as eligible counterparties:

- Investment firms.
- Credit institutions.
- Insurance companies.
- UCITS and their management companies.
- Pension funds and their management companies.
- Other financial institutions which are authorised or regulated according to EU law or the law of a member state.
- Commodity dealers and locals on stock exchanges.
- National governments and their respective executive organisations, including the public bodies which focus on the national debt.
- Central banks and supranational institutions.

The light touch regime only applies to specific types of business:

- Executing orders on behalf of clients.

- Dealing on own account.
- Receiving and transmitting orders.

If an eligible counterparty however does obtain investment advice, it should be treated as a professional client.

2. Professional clients

It is assumed that a professional client has sufficient knowledge, experience and expertise to be able to estimate independently which risks are attached to financial instruments and investment services. For this reason, this category of investors has a lower level of protection than retail investors and a number of rules of conduct are not applicable for professional customers.

MiFID automatically recognises the following entities as professional clients:

- Entities which are required to be authorised or regulated to operate in the financial markets, such as:
  - Credit institutions
  - Investment firms
  - Other authorised or regulated financial institutions
  - Insurance companies
  - Collective investment schemes and their management companies
  - Pension funds and their management companies
  - Commodity and commodity derivative dealers
  - Other institutional investors
- Large firms meeting two of the following three size requirements:
  - Balance sheet total of at least €20 million
  - Net turnover of at least €40 million
  - Equity of at least €2 million
- National and regional governments, public bodies that manage public debt, central banks and international and supranational institutions.
- Other institutional investors whose main activity is to invest in financial instruments, including entities dedicated to the securitisation of assets or other financing transactions.

Any clients not falling within the above list are, by default, retail clients.

3. Retail clients

Retail clients are investors who are not designated as professional clients or as eligible counterparties. Clients falling in the retail category are less experienced, knowledgeable and sophisticated investors and receive the most regulatory protection. For this category of customers, there are the largest number of rules in the area of communication, obligation to provide information and transparency.

MiFID requires that an investment firm must inform its customers as to the category to which they have been allocated, their right to request a different category and any limitations on protection that such a move would involve.

Change in customer classification

Clients can move between categories, which implies that the level of regulatory protection is increased or decreased. When a client requests a different categorisation, the investment firm has the choice whether to provide services on that basis or not. If the investment firm does not accept, the client will need to source services with the desired level of protection elsewhere. Investment firms can also unilaterally decide to treat all of their clients as retail clients if they want to, for instance for reasons of simplicity.

Below, I discuss the most important changes to the customer classification.

From retail to professional client

If a retail client wishes to become a professional client, the investment firm must assess whether the client has the necessary expertise, experience and knowledge and whether the client is capable of making his own investment decisions and risk assessment. The client must satisfy at least two of the following three criteria:

1. The client has carried out transactions, in significant size, on the relevant market at an average frequency of 10 per quarter over the previous four quarters.
2. The size of the client's financial instrument portfolio, defined as including cash deposits and financial instruments, exceeds €500,000.
3. The client works or has worked in the financial sector for at least one year in a professional position which requires knowledge of the transactions or services envisaged.

If a retail client wishes to be designated as a professional client by an investment firm, the following procedure must be followed:

- The investor makes a written request to this effect.
- The investment firm warns the customer in writing concerning the lower level of protection and the non-applicability of the investor compensation system.
- The customer sends written confirmation in a separate document that he is aware of the consequences related to the lower level of protection.

It will be specified in an agreement between the parties to which investment services, types of financial instruments or transactions the qualification as professional client will apply. If the investment firm observes that the client no longer complies structurally with the conditions to be eligible as a professional client, it must designate the client as a retail investor, and notify him to this effect.

From professional client to retail client

A professional client can request to be designated as a retail client. He will do so for instance if he feels he is unable to appropriately assess the risks involved and is looking for additional regulatory protection. An investment firm can designate a professional client as a retail client per investment service, per transaction or in general. If it is agreed that the professional investor is to be designated a non-professional investor, this is set down in a written agreement, in which it is determined to which investment services, types of financial instruments or transactions the qualification as retail client will apply.

From professional client to eligible counterparty

An investment firm can qualify a professional client as an eligible counterparty in general or with respect to specific transactions if it obtains a written request from its client.

From eligible counterparty to professional or retail client

An investment firm can treat an eligible counterparty as a professional or retail client, per transaction or in general, on request or at its own initiative.

Client suitability

It is an important obligation under MiFID for the investment firm to assess the client's suitability for certain investment products or services. This obligation depends on the type of relationship between the investment firm and its client. A key question is whether the investment firm provides investment advice, or services on the basis of execution only. This has to be clear to both parties from the beginning as the level of customer protection is distinctly different.

One of the elements of customer protection by investment firms is the 'know your customer principle'. For example, information about the customer's knowledge must contain data on the education, training and profession or the former profession of the customer. Investment firms must have access to information on the customer, known as the customer profile. The requirements under MiFID in this respect are based on the type of service or product:

- Investment advice
- Execution only

Investment advice

The starting point is that an investment firm that provides investment advice about derivatives to its client must ensure that it is suitable to the customer's level of experience, risk appetite and investment objectives. In order to do so, MiFID requires that the investment firm acquire information on its client's financial position, knowledge, experience, objectives and risk appetite, as far as this is relevant to the services provided. The investment firm must ensure that its provision of services is in line with the customer profile. The investment firm must clearly explain to the retail client how the advice fits with the client's goals. Futhermore, it should record this in writing so that collegues, internal compliance and external regulators are afterwards always able to identify why a certain derivative was advised. The level of the suitability test that investment firms have to carry out for investment advice differs for retail and professional clients.

Suitability of retail clients

An investment firm will have to weigh up, on a case-by-case basis, whether it has at its disposal the necessary information to enable it to evaluate the suitability of a transaction in a financial instrument for a customer. The following questions are important in the assessment of suitability for the customer:

- Are the investment objectives of the customer being met?
- Can the customer financially bear all the investment risks, in line with his investment objectives?
- In view of the customer's knowledge and experience, does he understand the investment risks attached to the transaction or to the management of his portfolio?

It may be the case in the context of the suitability test that some information on a specific element of the customer profile may be missing (if the customer does not have access to the requested information, but also if the customer deliberately withholds such information from an investment firm). It is not necessary for all the information to be available, on condition that the investment firm can reasonably be of the opinion that the missing information was not relevant to the evaluation of suitability.

Suitability of professional clients

In the case of advice to professional investors, the investment firm only needs to take into account the investment objectives of the customer. In such cases, the investment firm can assume that professional investors can financially bear investment risks and that they understand what risks are associated with transactions.

Execution only

Execution only means that the client asks an investment firm to buy or sell a derivative without the investment firm advising the client at the same time. For retail clients it should be clear from the start whether the investment firm advises the client or provides an execution only service. In some cases concerning retail clients the investment firm must test the appropriateness of the client for the proposed transaction. In the case of professional clients, the investment firm can assume that the customer has the necessary knowledge and experience, and no assessment of appropriateness is required.

In the sole case that a retail client approaches the investment firm on its own initiative and the relevant product is 'non-complex' (such as shares, bonds and rights of participation in an investment institution), the investment firm does not need to obtain any information from the customer and does not have to perform an appropriateness test. In all other cases the investment firm does have to check whether the proposed transaction is appropriate for the client.

The appropriateness test requires an investment firm to assess the client's knowledge and experience in the relevant investment field to establish whether the product provided is appropriate for the client.

An investment firm must take all reasonable measures in the execution of orders of financial instruments at the expense of customers to achieve the best possible result for them, taking into account a number of aspects. This is called 'best execution' and relates to the price of the financial instruments, the execution costs, the speed, the likelihood of execution and settlement, the size, nature and all other aspects relevant to the execution of the order.

Information provisioning

Providing sufficient information is a cornerstone of customer protection. Even in the case of execution only, the investment firm must provide sufficient information for the customer to be able to evaluate for himself whether the service or product fits. MiFID requires that the information to clients should be fair, clear and not misleading. We'll discuss the most important aspects with respect to the provision of information required by MiFID.

Timing of information

Investment firms must provide information to their customers in advance. Prior to the provision of services, an investment firm must provide the customer with information that is reasonably relevant in the context of an adequate assessment of the service or product. The information referred to can be provided in a standardised form. In addition, marketing material and other information provided must not be deleterious to the information to be provided compulsorily. All information provided by the investment firm, including advertising, must be correct, clear and not misleading.

The information to be provided in advance must contain a general description of the major risks of financial instruments which is detailed enough to enable a retail client to take an investment decision.

Information on inducements

An investment firm must work in an honest, fair and professional manner for its customers in the provision of investment services and ancillary services. Fees which an investment firm receives or pays can have a major influence on this. For this reason, the basic principle is that the investment firm does not pay or receive any fees for the provision of an investment service unless the payments are necessary for the provision of the investment service in question, or make it possible. These could include a custody fee, interchange fees and stock exchange fees, statutory levies or legal fees. In the case of such payments, the investment firm must look after the customer's interests in a loyal, fair and professional manner.

Supplementary to the above, fees which the investment firm receives from the customer himself, or passes on to the customer, are also permissible. In this way, the investment firm can be certain that the customer is aware of the level of the fees.

Fees must be made transparent for the customer in terms of their existence, nature and level. The fees must also not be deleterious to the investment firm's efforts on behalf of the customer, and must also benefit the quality of the provision of services. As the application of the rule on fees is extremely complex, CESR has drawn up a document which can serve as a guideline in the assessment of the permissibility of a number of fees.

Information recorded in writing

Investment firms must draw up a customer agreement on paper or on another long-term medium for the performance of investment services and any ancillary services. Such a customer agreement must guarantee that customers of investment firms and the investment firms themselves are aware of what they are involved in, that it is clear what the rights and obligations of both parties are and which investment services are being provided in which manner.

The customer agreement forms the basis for the provision of investment services by the investment firm to the customer. This has no effect, however, on the fact that one or more of the subjects which must form part of the customer agreement, such as the permission for the execution of orders outside a regulated market or MTF, can be set down in a separate agreement. One condition in this respect is that this separate agreement forms part of the customer agreement by means of a reference.

Custody period information storage

MiFID requires an investment firm to retain all relevant data on transactions with its customers in financial instruments for at least five years. The reason for this is that the financial regulator can assess, in retrospect, whether the investment firm has acted honestly, fairly, professionally and in a manner which is not harmful to integrity when entering into transactions.

MIFID II

MiFID came into force on 1 November 2007. In order to close the holes in MiFID and in response to the financial crisis and reforms in the financial markets it will be succeeded by MiFID II. Investment firms in the EU member states must be fully compliant with MiFID II by 2 January 2017. I'll discuss some of the most important changes under MiFID II with respect to derivatives and customer protection.

In order to improve customer protection, the requirements with respect to the provision of information by investment firms to their customers are enhanced under MiFID II. MiFID II now clearly articulates that investment firms must tailor the design, marketing and distribution of products to their specific target markets. Furthermore, when an investment firm bundles products or services it must tell its clients whether the individual components can be purchased separately.

MiFID II is more specific regarding the provision of information on costs to the customer. Where investment firms bundle products or services, they should provide evidence of the costs and charges for each component separately. Information regarding costs and associated charges must relate to both investment and ancillary services and must include the cost of advice, the cost of the financial instrument and how the client may pay for it, and any third party payments. Information about costs and charges, which are not caused by underlying market risk, must be aggregated, with a breakdown per item provided at the client's request. This information must be provided to the client at least annually during the life of the investment.

MiFID II also enhances the requirements with respect to investment advisors. Investment firms will have to ensure and demonstrate to regulators that advisors possess the necessary knowledge and competence to fulfil their obligations. Also, it is now specifically required that remuneration and sales targets should not incentivise staff to recommend inappropriate financial instruments to retail clients.

Notes

Chapter 1 Key learning points from past derivatives blunders

1. Roel Janssen, 'Grof geld: Financiële schandalen en speculatie in Nederland', De bezige bij, November 2012. ISBN 978–90–234–7789–1. The book is available in Dutch only.
2. Stefan Aust and Thomas Ammann, 'Die Porsche Saga: eine Familiëngeschichte des Automobils', Quadriga, 2012. ISBN 978–3-86995–014–3. This is a fascinating book about (sports) cars, success, money and power. Unfortunately, currently it is only available in German.
3. *The Economist*: Squeezy money, 'How Porsche fleeced hedge funds and roiled the world's financial markets', www.economist.com/node/12523898.

Chapter 4 The financial markets

1. As from 2014 the following members of the European Union (EU) use the euro: Austria, Belgium, Cyprus, Estonia, Finland, France, Germany, Greece, Ireland, Italy, Latvia, Luxembourg, Malta, The Netherlands, Portugal, Slovenia, Slovakia and Spain. The following members of the EU do not use the euro: Bulgaria, Czech Republic, Denmark, Croatia, Lithuania, Hungary, Poland, Romania, Sweden and the United Kingdom (www.ecb.europa.eu).
2. The figure illustrating the ECB refinancing rate is from www.ecb.europa.eu on 12 September 2014.
3. The figure illustrating the Fed fund rate is from www.fedprimerate.com on 12 September 2014.
4. The table showing the interest rates of central banks around the world is from www.global-rates.com on 9 September 2014.
5. The panel of banks contributing to Euribor consists of 26 banks: Belfius from Belgium; Nordea and Pohjola from Finland; BNP Parisbas, HSBC France, Natixis, Crédit Agricole and Société Générale from France; Deutsche Bank, Commerzbank and DZ Bank from Germany; National Bank of Greece from Greece; Intesa Sanpaolo, Monte dei Paschi di Siena and UniCredit from Italy; Banque et Caisse d'Epargne de l'Etat from Luxembourg; ING Bank from the Netherlands; Caixa Geral De Depósitos from Portugal; Banco Bilbao Vizcaya Argentaria, Banco Santander, CECABANK and CaixaBank from Spain; Barclays Capital and Den Danske Bank as other EU banks; London branch of JP Morgan Chase Bank and Bank of Tokyo Mitsubishi as international banks (www.emmi-benchmarkts.eu).
6. The figure illustrating a snapshot in time of the Euribor rates is from www.global-rates.com on 12 September 2014.

7. The figure illustrating 3-months Euribor over time from its inception is from www.global-rates.com.
8. The figure illustrating a snapshot in time of different LIBOR rates is from www.global-rates.com on 12 September 2014.
9. The figure illustrating the euro and USD capital market yield curve is from www.ecb.europa.eu and www.treasury.gov on 11 September 2014.

Chapter 6 Hedging makes sense under specific circumstances only

1. F. Modigliani and M.H. Miller, 'The cost of capital, corporation finance and the theory of investment', *The American Economic Review* 48 (1958), 261–92.
2. M.H. Miller, 'The Modigliani-Miller propositions after thirty years', *Journal of Economic Perspectives* 2 (1998), 99–120.
3. The table showing progressive corporate taxes in various countries is from KPMG: http://www.kpmg.com/global/en/services/tax/tax-tools-and-resources/pages/corporate-tax-rates-table.aspx

Chapter 8 Linear derivatives

1. The table showing the worldwide OTC market for swaps and FRAs is from the Bank of International Settlements (BIS).

Chapter 9 Options

1. The table showing the worldwide OTC market for options is from the BIS.

Glossary

Ask price The lowest price a seller is willing to accept. Also called offer price.

Bid price The highest price a buyer is willing to pay.

Bullet loan A loan where the entire repayment is due at the end of the term.

Cap An option in which the holder (buyer) receives interest payments at the end of each period in which the reference rate exceeds the pre-agreed strike price.

Capital market The part of the financial market for borrowing and lending money for terms longer than one year. Interest rates in the capital market are a result of supply and demand and can barely be influenced by central banks. The interest rates in the capital market determine the interest on loans for firms.

Cash and cash equivalents A cash balance in the current account and cash that is placed in the money market, such as time deposits or other money market products. They can be converted to cash quickly. Cash can be used for repaying debt. In order to calculate a firm's net debt position cash is therefore subtracted from interest-bearing liabilities.

Collar A combination of buying a cap and selling a floor (long collar) or vice versa (short collar). The firm buying a cap maximises interest payable (the cap strike). In order to lower the option premium of the cap, the firm at the same time sells a floor. As a result of the floor the firm settles for a certain minimum interest payable (the floor strike).

Corporate financial risk management The management at non-financial firms of interest rate risk, foreign exchange risk and commodity risk.

Counterparty risk The risk that a counterparty in a financial contract defaults on its obligations during the term of the contract. By nature both counterparties are exposed to it, but only in the case that the contract has a positive value.

Debt service The combination of interest and debt redemption payments.

Default A situation where a firm fails to meet the interest and debt redemption obligations of a financing arrangement.

Derivative A contract that derives its value from the performance of an underlying interest rate. Common derivatives are futures, swaps and options.

Dividend The part of a firm's net profits which is distributed to its shareholders.

Euribor Euribor is short for Euro Interbank Offered rate and was created in 1999 with the introduction of the euro. Euribor rates are based on the average interest rates at which a panel of 26 European banks borrow unsecured funds from one another in the euro interbank market. Euribor is determined and published around 11 a.m. each day. There are eight different Euribor rates with maturities ranging from one week to one year.

Exchange-traded derivative Standardised derivative contract (e.g. futures and options) that is traded on a regulated exchange.

Financial covenants A financial covenant is a ratio. The term 'financial covenant' is used as soon as the ratio is included in a financing arrangement as a covenant. Once this happens, there are consequences involved if the covenant is broken. In principle, the bank is entitled to call in the facility immediately in such a situation. Examples of common financial covenants are: solvency ratio, Interest Coverage Ratio (ICR), net debt / EBITDA ratio and Debt Service Coverage Ratio (DSCR).

Financial distress A situation in which a firm has insufficient cash to pay its financial obligations to third parties, such as payments for goods and services to its creditors, interest and debt repayment to its bank or salaries to its employees. Avoiding a situation of financial distress is an important reason for firms to hedge interest rate risk.

Financial non-current assets These can include interest-bearing positions such as loans to third parties for which interest is received. They may also include non-interest-bearing positions such as participating interests in other firms.

Fixed rate loan The interest rate of the loan is fixed over the full tenure of the loan. As a result a firm is not exposed to interest rate risk as the interest payments due in the future are known upfront.

Floor An option contract in which the buyer receives interest payments at the end of each period in which the reference rate is below the pre-agreed strike price.

FRA An FRA (Forward Rate Agreement) is a contract between two parties to determine the rate of interest to be paid or received over a notional principal amount at a future start date. A firm buying an FRA locks in a reference money market rate in order to protect itself from an interest rate increase, while a firm selling an FRA protects itself from an interest rate decrease.

Future A financial contract to buy or sell a standardised amount of an underlying instrument at a future date and at a pre-agreed price.

Hedge A transaction that offsets an underlying position and reduces risk.

Interest-bearing assets Sources of exposure to interest rate risk for a firm that can be found on the asset side of the balance sheet: cash and cash equivalents and financial non-current assets.

Interest-bearing liabilities Sources of exposure to interest rate risk for a firm that can be found on the liability side of the balance sheet: short-term loans and long-term loans.

Interest rate risk A firm is exposed to interest rate risk if it has interest-bearing assets or liabilities and if the interest rate on these positions is variable. This is because the firm is uncertain about the level of interest receipts or payments due in the future.

Interest rate swap A derivative in which two parties agree to exchange interest rate cash flows, based on a pre-agreed notional principal amount, from a variable rate to a fixed rate or vice versa.

LIBOR London Interbank Offered Rate. It is the average interest rate that leading banks in London are charged when borrowing from one another. LIBOR is a benchmark for worldwide short-term interest rates and is also used as a basis for pricing derivatives transactions and loans to firms.

Linear derivatives Instruments that fix the interest rate. As a result the firm has certainty about the interest payable in the future (excluding the markup). Linear derivatives are like forward contracts: parties agree on settling the difference between an agreed interest rate and the prevailing market interest rate in the future. Interest rate swaps and FRAs (forward rate agreements) are key linear derivatives.

Long-term loans Loans with a remaining term of more than one year. The portion of a long-term loan that is repaid within a period of a year is administered under short-term loans. In principle all long-term loans are interest-bearing.

Modigliani and Miller In 1958 Modigliani and Miller argue that in a perfect capital market the market value of a firm is unaffected by its capital structure decisions because they can be replicated by investors. Later this is extended to hedging. In modern corporate finance theory their framework still serves as an important benchmark: it shows how a firm can benefit from managing interest rate risk if the conditions assumed by Modigliani and Miller are relaxed in the light of market imperfections.

Money market The part of the financial market for borrowing and lending money with terms between one day and one year. Only very large parties, such as banks, governments, institutional investors and very large firms have direct access to the money market. The money market, however, is basically an interbank market. Central banks can influence prices in the money market.

Open derivatives position A situation where a firm has a derivative without an underlying asset or liability.

Option A contract between two parties that gives the buyer the right, but not the obligation, to buy or sell a specific instrument at a specified price on or before a specific future date. When the buyer exercises the option, the seller must deliver, or take delivery of the underlying instrument at the specified price. The buyer pays an option premium to the seller for this right.

Option premium The cost of an option contract which the buyer pays to the seller. The option premium depends on the intrinsic value of the option and on the time value.

Overhedging A situation where an open derivatives position arises without an underlying asset or liability. Overhedging can occur because of a mismatch between the principal or the term of a derivative and those of the underlying exposure.

Over-the-counter (OTC) A bilateral, tailor-made, transaction between a firm and a bank.

Short-term loans Loans with a term of less than one year. They are part of current liabilities. Some current liabilities are interest-bearing, such as a current account overdraft. Some current liabilities are non-interest-bearing, such as creditors, tax payable and prepayments.

Solvency An important measure to assess whether a firm is able to survive in the long term. As a result solvency is often used as a financial covenant in financing agreements. Solvency is often linked to a firm's ability to borrow: the higher its solvency, the more potential a firm has to raise new loan capital.

Speculation The intention is to take a gamble with derivatives based on a personal view of future interest rate movements. Risk is knowingly taken by entering into an open derivatives position without an underlying position.

Strike price The fixed price at which the option holder has the right to buy (cap) or sell (floor) the underlying instrument. Also called exercise price.

Swaption An option into a predetermined interest rate swap transaction.

Variable interest rate Interest on an interest-bearing asset or liability that is not fixed over its life. Also known as floating interest rate.

Volatility A measure for the variation of the price over time.

Yield curve A yield curve, also called term structure of interest rates, depicts the interest rates for debt with different maturities but with the same risk.

Index

Page numbers in **bold** or *italics* refer to glossary definitions and figures respectively. The suffix T indicates a table, and *box* indicates boxed material.